Who Needs the BANK?

Why you should <u>BE</u> a bank instead of investing in one!

OR

How to earn 5 to 50 times more than banks pay by investing in loans to hard-working, self-employed business owners whom the banks turn down

Bob Zachmeier

Out of the Box Books
Tucson, Arizona

This publication contains the opinions, ideas, and personal experiences of its author. It is sold with the understanding that neither the author nor the publisher is engaged in rendering legal, tax, investment, insurance, financial, accounting, or other professional advice or services. If the reader requires such advice or services, a competent professional should be consulted. Relevant laws vary from state to state. The strategies outlined in this book may not be suitable for every individual, and are not guaranteed or warranted to produce any particular results. No warranty is made with respect to the accuracy or completeness of the information contained herein, and both the author and the publisher specifically disclaim any responsibility for any liability, loss, or risk, personal or otherwise, which is incurred as a consequence, directly or indirectly, of the use and application of any of the contents of this book.

Copyright © 2018 by Bob Zachmeier

All rights reserved, including the right of reproduction in whole or in part in any form.

ISBN: 978-0-9801855-6-0

Library of Congress Control Number: 2018910695

For information on other books by Bob Zachmeier, visit the publisher's website at: www.outoftheboxbooks.com

When it comes to books… think Out of the Box!

Out of the Box Books
P.O. Box 64878, Tucson, AZ 85728

For Bill and BettyJo Zachmeier

I was blessed to have parents who wouldn't allow me to give up when problems arose. Dad taught me to take things apart to understand how they work and then find a way to fix them. Mom taught me to think "out of the box" to find creative alternatives that could accomplish the same task. Together, they've enabled their confident and creative children to lead successful and happy lives by constantly challenging norms to find "win-win-win" solutions that make the world a better place.

"Creativity is not just for artists, it's for businesspeople looking for a new way to close a sale, for engineers trying to solve a problem, and for parents who want their children to see the world in more than one way.

- *Twyla Tharp*

TABLE OF CONTENTS

ACKNOWLEDGEMENTS	ix
INTRODUCTION	xi
CHAPTER 1 – Why Do People Need Loans?	1
CHAPTER 2 – Why Won't Banks Make the Loans?	5
CHAPTER 3 – Aren't These People "Deadbeats?"	11
CHAPTER 4 – What If They Don't Repay Me?	17
CHAPTER 5 – What Documentation is Needed?	21
CHAPTER 6 – Aren't Banks "Safe" Investments?	27
CHAPTER 7 – How Do Notes Compare to Banks?	33
CHAPTER 8 – Should Baby Boomers Buy Notes?	39
CHAPTER 9 – Are Notes Better Than Stocks?	43
CHAPTER 10 – Are Notes Better Than Rentals?	47
CHAPTER 11 How Do I Compare Investments?	51
CHAPTER 12 – Are Notes Better Investments?	55
CHAPTER 13 – How Do I Qualify the Borrower?	59
CHAPTER 14 – Will I Become a Bill Collector?	65

TABLE OF CONTENTS

CHAPTER 15 – How Do I Set the Interest Rate?   71

CHAPTER 16 – What If I'm Not Ready to Retire?   77

CHAPTER 17 – What If I Need Income Now?   83

CHAPTER 18 – What If I Need to Sell My Notes?   89

CHAPTER 19 – What If I Die Before I'm Repaid?   95

CHAPTER 20 – Where Can I Find Notes to Fund?   101

CHAPTER 21 – What Should I Look For In Notes?   107

CHAPTER 22 – How Can I Get Started With Notes?   113

CHAPTER 23 – Why Do I Need to Start Right Away?   119

CHAPTER 24 – How Can I Learn More About Notes?   125

CHAPTER 25 – Note Investing Success Story   131

How to Find Out More About Notes   135

About the Author   136

TABLE OF CONTENTS

Figures in This Book

6-1	Federal Reserve Home Price Index	30
7-1	Loan Comparison	34
7-2	Negative Interest Rates	36
9-1	Market Cap to GDP	46
10-1	Monthly Rental Property Expenses	49
11-1	The Rule of 72	53
12-1	Loan to Value Over Time	58
14-1	7-Year Foreclosure Completion Rate	67
14-2	Years to Save for a 10% Down Payment	69
16-1	Median Seller Tenure	78
16-2	Notes Accumulated	79
16-3	Note Amortization Schedule	80
18-1	Amortized Loan Balance	91
18-2	Note Buyer Yield of 5%	92
18-3	Note Buyer Yield of 7%	93
23-1	Compound Interest on $100,000	122
24-1	Trailer Park Sale History	127

ACKNOWLEDGEMENTS

I thank God for blessing me with the ability to attract amazing people into my life. I've prevailed through many challenges due to the love and support of family and friends.

I thank my wife, Camille, who spent many evenings and weekends alone while I've worked on my books and NoteCarry software. Her hard work and attention to detail has enabled us to close more than 4,000 home sales. Camille is smart, fun, and an awesome partner in business and life.

I thank my parents who taught me to see things as they *could be* rather than as they are. Their *vision* and optimism are alive and well in me today. Dad passed away in 1996, but Mom continues to impact my life. She used flashcards to help me pass 3rd grade when I struggled with multiplication, was my business partner in a fireworks stand in 10th grade, and has been the chief proofreader on all six of my books.

I thank my Scoutmaster, Val Heck, and all of the adult volunteers who donated hundreds of hours to help me earn the 36 merit badges required to become an Eagle Scout. My life is a collection of experiences made possible by generations of people who've given freely of their time, talents, and financial resources to benefit others. Their compassion for their fellow human beings sets an example for the rest of us to follow.

I thank my brother, Mike, for bringing a unique and valuable perspective to our real estate business for 10 years. He got straight A's his entire life and always made me look bad, but his attention to detail has often come in handy! He also does an awesome job at catching mistakes in my books.

I thank Craig and Catherine Proctor for their real estate strategies that helped us close over 600 homes per year, more

ACKNOWLEDGEMENTS

than average agents close in a lifetime! Many of the real estate agents they've attracted have become our closest friends.

I thank Tom and Naomi Moon for REObroker.com, a network of caring people with a *pay it forward* attitude. Their support of my fundraising endeavors is truly appreciated.

I thank Alan and Joan Langston for the opportunity to speak at Arizona Real Estate Investor's Association (AZREIA) meetings since 2004. The new ideas they continue to introduce have helped thousands of new and experienced investors.

I thank Eddie Speed for making me think differently about real estate financing. His note training came just in time when few could qualify for bank loans after the recession.

I thank Walter Wofford for his creative investment strategies and willingness to share his knowledge with others. If you look up *southern hospitality* in the dictionary, you're certain to find a photo of Walter and his beautiful wife, Laura.

I thank H. Quincy Long, CEO of Quest Trust Company, for using his unique skill set to teach others how to create a better retirement. Quincy is probably the only person in the country who is an experienced title company attorney, has owned a tax preparation franchise, founded an IRA custodial company, and understands creative investment strategies. He and his wife, Marsha, have a passion for helping people save.

I thank my business partner, Kelly Anne Porter, for her behind-the scene efforts on our investment deals and the endless hours spent working in my booth at note conferences.

I thank Yolanda Estrada for helping me keep all the "balls in the air" on my local deals, Simon White, Francisco Estrada, and Nand Kishor for their help to develop NoteCarry.com, and the members of the NoteCarry Network who've placed their trust in me to mentor them about notes and note investing.

INTRODUCTION

Travel to the largest cities in the world and you'll find that the tallest buildings often have the name of a bank on their side. How can banks afford such expensive real estate? From the fees and interest they receive from loans.

Homeowners who obtain a mortgage can expect to pay 2% to 5% of their home's purchase price in lender fees. On a $200,000 home these fees would range between $4,000.00 and $10,000.00. When multiplied by the 50 million mortgages in the United States, the *loan fees* are between $200 billion and $500 billion dollars, but that's just the tip of the iceberg!

In addition to the fees paid to initiate loans, banks collect interest every month for 30 years. If the home is sold before the loan is repaid, the process starts all over again with more fees and more interest.

Buyers pay the fees and interest charged by banks because they don't have a choice. If they want to own a home and don't have the cash, they either pay the fees and interest or don't get the loan.

Unfortunately, the huge profits earned by banks aren't being passed on to their depositors. Record profits are being made on the backs of retired people who can't afford the lifestyle they worked their entire lives to achieve, but it doesn't have to be that way. Since the fees and interest are going to be paid to *someone*, why shouldn't they be paid to *you*?

INTRODUCTION

This book is filled with information and real life examples of people who are beating the banks at their own game. To learn how you can earn 5 to 50 times more than the interest offered by your bank, read on!

The information in this book may challenge beliefs that you've held for decades. I encourage you to set your long-held beliefs aside and open your mind to new possibilities. The most expensive thing you can own is a *closed mind!*

Enjoy!

1

Why Do People Need Loans?

"Capital is that part of wealth which is devoted to obtaining further wealth."

- Alfred Marshall

WHO NEEDS THE BANK?

People in the United States enjoy the highest standard of living in the world because of the abundance of credit. Credit gives us the opportunity to buy the things we need before we have the money to pay for them.

If we couldn't buy a car or home until we had the money to pay for them, we'd be forced to walk everywhere and live in the tents we could afford to pay cash for at Wal-Mart. Without access to credit, the United States would be like third world countries that don't offer the opportunity for credit to their citizens.

Credit is an enabler. It enables us to obtain a car loan, which enables us to commute, which enables us to take higher paying jobs in areas much farther than we'd be able to walk to in a day.

Our homes offer security, comfort, and shelter from the elements, enabling us to sleep better and be more productive at our jobs. That productivity enables us to earn higher wages, and thus provide better food, clothing, shelter, and a higher standard of living for our families.

Through years of experience in dealing with a variety of problems, I've found a niche in private financing and have created, tested, perfected, and shared several unique programs to help people across the country buy and sell homes.

Sellers who don't have loans on their homes can offer financing for their buyers, but those who have loans may not be able to become the bank for their buyers.

CHAPTER 1 – WHY DO PEOPLE NEED LOANS?

The benefits of private financing for the buyer, seller, and investor are provided below:

BUYER BENEFITS

Buyers get a home that traditional lenders won't allow them to have. Instead of paying off their landlord's mortgage, they can create their own wealth through the American dream of home ownership. The monthly payment to *own* a home is often less than the cost of rent, creating an immediate cash surplus for the borrower every month.

In addition to a lower monthly payment, homeowners can usually deduct mortgage interest and property tax to reduce the amount they owe in income tax. The additional tax deductions can increase the amount of their paycheck, adding even more to their monthly cash surplus.

Home equity is achieved through principal reduction on each monthly payment and market appreciation. These are long-term benefits that won't be realized until the home is sold but often account for over *half* of a homeowner's net worth at retirement. None of these benefits can be achieved by renting.

SELLER BENEFITS

Sellers who finance their buyer typically receive a higher price and their homes sell faster. The appreciative buyers tend to ask for few if any repairs after the home inspection. In addition to selling their homes for more money in less time with the least hassle, owners who finance earn a much higher interest rate than banks or other investments pay.

WHO NEEDS THE BANK?

Sellers can also experience tax benefits by taking their profit from the sale of their home over *time* instead of receiving it in one lump sum. The safety and flexibility of loans secured by real estate make the investments easy to sell.

Landlords who sell their properties and finance their buyers often receive more each month from owning the *paper* than they ever received while owning the *property* and they avoid the "tenant and toilet" hassles of being a landlord.

INVESTOR BENEFITS

When sellers are unwilling or unable to finance the home they're selling, we access our list of past clients and retirees interested in deploying their funds in another investment. Many retirees don't think of themselves as real estate investors because they've never owned rental properties, but when they finance notes secured by real estate, they become real estate investors.

Most of the retirees who fund real estate notes for our clients have their cash sitting in a bank earning little or no interest. They're willing to lend to complete strangers because they can earn exponentially higher returns on loans secured by the borrower's home.

It's common for our investors and retirees to earn 5 to 50 times more than the interest they receive from their bank! For over a decade, retired people have enjoyed a better lifestyle by helping our clients purchase homes. This is a true *win-win-win* scenario.

2

Why Won't Banks Make the Loans?

"A banker is a fellow who lends you his umbrella when the sun is shining, but wants it back the minute it begins to rain."
— *Mark Twain*

WHO NEEDS THE BANK?

Prior to the financial market meltdown in 2008 the government seemed to adopt the belief that home ownership was the Constitutional right of every American. They pressured banks to lower the qualification criteria so more people could obtain loans. Soon anyone who could "fog a mirror" (was alive and breathing) could qualify for a loan.

What followed was the worst financial collapse since the Great Depression. Six million loans went into default and banks were foreclosing in record numbers. As foreclosure homes flooded the market with deeply discounted homes, property values began to free-fall. Buyers stopped purchasing homes and sat on the fence, waiting for the market to bottom as home values and interest rates plummeted for years.

With few buyers, banks had price-lowering contests with one another. They needed to sell the homes they'd foreclosed on but few buyers were willing to purchase them. As prices continued to decline, more and more homeowners were "under water," owing more than the market value of their home.

With an overabundance of homes and a shortage of buyers to purchase them, Congress responded by passing the Dodd-Frank Act. This legislation, the collaborative effort of Christopher Dodd and Barney Frank, made it even harder for buyers to obtain a mortgage and created severe penalties for lenders who provided loans to borrowers who later defaulted.

The legislation may have started as a noble attempt to curb the unscrupulous lending practices that caused the

CHAPTER 2 – WHY WON'T BANKS MAKE THE LOANS?

financial meltdown, but what resulted were laws so restrictive and with such severe penalties that few banks and private lenders were willing to offer loans at all!

According to Ellie Mae, a software company that processes almost a quarter of all U.S. mortgage applications, banks turned down nearly half of all mortgage applications in the United States in 2014. That statistic doesn't include all of the buyers who didn't apply because they knew they'd be declined for a loan. How could home prices ever recover if lenders wouldn't approve half the buyers who apply for loans?

Investors came to the rescue to stop the free fall in home values. While traditional buyers were waiting for the market to bottom, it was investors who determined that the market had fallen enough to make a profit. If investors hadn't jumped in to buy the surplus homes when they did, values would still be falling and buyers would still be waiting for the bottom!

Due to the purchases by investors, prices began to stabilize in 2011. Several months later, traditional buyers returned to the market when the newspapers reported that home values had increased and they'd *missed the bottom!* The investors who had the courage to invest when few others were buying got the best deals. The market turned around and home values rose sharply when the fence-sitting buyers stormed the market after a four-year hiatus.

During the period when banks wouldn't lend, investors saved the day again by offering loans to the qualified borrowers that the banks turned down.

WHO NEEDS THE BANK?

Real estate investors can also be credited with increasing neighborhood values because they buy the least expensive homes, then renovate and resell them. The newly transformed homes sell at the highest prices in the area and when the sale is recorded, the price will be used as a reference every time another home is listed, appraised, or sold. This establishes a higher market value for other homes in the neighborhood.

Banks are in the business of providing loans, but most sell the loans as soon as they're funded to generate the capital to fund more loans. The loans are bundled into packages with other loans and sold to Fannie Mae, Freddie Mac, large banks, insurance companies, or hedge funds which are collectively referred to as the *secondary market*.

These loan-buying entities require certain criteria of the loans that they purchase, which often include consistent income, length of time on the job, and no gaps in employment. Every month, banks turn down thousands of qualified borrowers, including many self-employed business owners who possess a very strong work ethic and earn far more than an average borrower.

These borrowers have saved for their down payment and can easily afford the monthly payments, but often don't fit within the bank's lending criteria because:
1) their income isn't consistent every month
2) they work on tips or are paid in cash
3) they take too many income tax deductions
4) they don't have two years in their business

CHAPTER 2 – WHY WON'T BANKS MAKE THE LOANS?

People aren't always the problem, sometimes it's the *property*. We recently funded a borrower with an 800 credit score who purchased a 1969 mobile home on land for $50,000. The borrower had owned a mobile home on a rented lot for 21 years, worked at the same job for 17 years, and had saved $20,000 for the down payment (40% of the purchase price).

Banks couldn't lend the $30,000 this highly-qualified borrower needed for the purchase because of the age of the mobile home and the amount of the loan. The Dodd-Frank Act limits the fees banks can charge to 5% of the loan amount.

This may sound good in theory, but on a $30,000 loan, the fees would be limited to $1,500, which is about the cost of the underwriting, processing, and appraisal for the loan. This leaves no room for banks to earn a profit, which means people who wish to purchase lower-priced properties can no longer obtain the financing to do so. Again, investors save the day!

WHO NEEDS THE BANK?

3

Aren't These People "Deadbeats?"

"I was never a big-company type of person, and my ideal job was to be self-employed. The ironic thing is you work a lot harder for yourself than you do for anybody else."

— Xochi Birch

WHO NEEDS THE BANK?

It's a mistake to assume that those who can't get loans from banks are irresponsible or unreliable people who don't honor their obligation to repay their debts. Although that might be true of some people, it's certainly not the case with many of the borrowers being declined by banks.

Few self-employed business owners I know work a 40-hour week. In fact, most work twice that many hours if not more! Don't you find it odd that many of the hardest working people in America can't qualify for a loan? These borrowers are not unemployed "deadbeats" who don't pay their bills. Many don't meet the bank's qualification criteria because they're self-employed, own too many properties, recently graduated from college, or have less than two years at their job. Do any of these things indicate that the borrowers won't repay their loans?

Borrowers who obtain private financing often have three times more down payment than bank-approved buyers. They're willing to pay a higher purchase price to homeowners who offer financing because they can't borrow from a bank.

Business owners aren't usually declined because of their credit; they're often turned down because they have irregular income that comes in *spurts*. Most businesses have cycles, with high seasons and low seasons; profitable months and unprofitable months and banks don't like that!

Bank loans are designed for those who have consistent, verifiable W-2 income paid by an employer every two weeks. Most self-employed people don't earn at the same predictable

CHAPTER 3 – AREN'T THESE PEOPLE "DEADBEATS?"

wage every two weeks and thus don't fit in the bank's box. These borrowers are often rejected, unable to achieve their dream of home ownership unless they can find a private lender to provide the financing they need.

Banks clamor to lend to the borrowers who require government assistance for their down payment and the home seller to pay their closing costs. Without any savings, these "qualified" borrowers would struggle to pay for even small repairs, such as a water heater, and would certainly be unable to afford major expenses such as roof replacement.

Why would banks offer government-backed loans to people with no money and no proven ability to save while turning down business owners with substantially higher income, a sizeable savings account, and a multitude of other assets? This question defies logic, and I've learned that you can't put *logic* in the same sentence as *bank* or *government*. This void in the bank's lending process creates a tremendous opportunity for those willing to fill it!

After considering all of these factors, I've come to the conclusion that many borrowers whom the banks turn down are better credit risks than those they approve!

During the Great Recession of 2008, our small real estate brokerage in Tucson, AZ, sold more than 2,000 bank-owned homes. In June, 2011, we sold 62 homes in 30 days; a sale every 11.6 hours. But as prices began to increase, the steady stream of foreclosed properties ended abruptly and I had to find another niche in the real estate market.

WHO NEEDS THE BANK?

About that time, an employee who was a single mom arrived at work in a new minivan. The woman was struggling to raise two kids on her own and her old, unreliable car seemed to always be in the shop for repairs. We'd discussed her financial situation on several occasions and she confided that she was unable to obtain financing for a newer car.

When I asked how she was able to purchase the minivan, she explained that she'd seen an advertisement for a sale at a local dealership. When they saw the car she was trading in, they informed her that they could not offer the sale price and she'd have to pay full sticker price. Due to the balance still owed on her car, she had no equity and agreed to a loan at 19.9% interest! The high interest rate made the payments higher than she could afford so the dealer extended the term to 7 years to lower the payment.

As I stood horrified, processing the transaction she'd just described, she broke into a huge smile and reached out to "high five" me saying, "But they gave me the car!"

I couldn't stop thinking about how the auto dealership had taken advantage of this poor woman! Throughout the day I watched as she showed off her new minivan to agents, staff, and anyone else who came into our office. I'd never seen her as happy or excited!

As I pondered how she could possibly be excited about striking such a terrible deal, I recalled that in addition to the never-ending repair bills, she was still making monthly loan payments on her previous car. I calculated the payment on the

CHAPTER 3 – AREN'T THESE PEOPLE "DEADBEATS?"

new minivan and concluded that even with the 19.9% interest rate, the payment was less than she'd been spending on her old, unreliable car.

The new minivan had a two-year warranty, eliminating the chance of expensive repairs and it was more fuel efficient, saving her money at the gas pump every week. The new vehicle was safe and reliable; reducing the chance that she and her kids would be stranded on the side of the road and it was hard not to notice how much the new vehicle increased her self esteem. Although it would be a horrible deal for me, I realized that the purchase was actually a *good deal* for her!

As I drifted off to sleep that night, I began to think of how the same rationale could help credit-challenged buyers purchase homes.

WHO NEEDS THE BANK?

4

What If They Don't Repay Me?

"I don't care if it's a dollar or two dollars. If I'm governor, people should have skin in the game."

- Matt Bevin

WHO NEEDS THE BANK?

An obvious question asked by people who are new to private financing is, "What if the borrower doesn't repay me?" This is a legitimate question as many of the people who invest with us are retired and no longer have the ability to replace lost capital. To protect the retiree lending partners who invest with us, we record their loan in 1st position at no more than 80% of the property's value and take a 2nd position loan behind them.

For example, if a buyer purchases a home valued at $100,000, the retiree's 1st position loan wouldn't exceed $80,000. If the borrower makes a $10,000 cash down payment, the remaining $10,000 of the purchase price would come from a 2nd position loan of $10,000. I often fund these loans since I can easily find another buyer if the original loan defaults.

If the borrower doesn't repay the loans as promised, they lose their $10,000 down payment. If I don't initiate a foreclosure action and make up the missing payments to the 1st position lien holder, I'd lose my $10,000 investment in the 2nd position note.

Creating two loans significantly lowers the risk for the retirees in 1st position. If there were a market downturn, the property would have to lose more than 20% of its value before the collateral would fall below the value of the 1st position loan.

If something unforeseen happens to the borrower and a lender needs to foreclose, the loan balance would be lower due to payments already made and the property's value would likely be higher due to appreciation over time.

CHAPTER 4 – WHAT IF THEY DON"T REPAY ME?

How many investments do you have that could lose 20% of their value without any loss of principal or interest? I encourage you to contact your stock broker and ask them to partner with you to buy 100 shares of stock. Tell them that you'll buy 80 shares if they'll buy the other 20, but if the market falls, their shares would be lost before your shares are affected.

Somehow, I don't think a stockbroker or many other people would go for that deal, but that's exactly what I offer to my investing partners! I'm willing to take a 2nd position loan behind them because the borrower is behind me with a lot of "skin" in the game from their down payment.

How long do you think it would take a person buying a $100,000 home to save $10,000 for the down payment? Several *years*, which means they're not likely to walk away and lose their substantial down payment.

In the rare event that the borrower is injured, killed, or otherwise unable to pay, the lien holder in 2nd position would likely catch up the missing payments and late fees to the 1st lien holder to protect their investment until the property can be foreclosed on and sold to another borrower.

In the event the 2nd lien holder is unwilling or unable to foreclose, the 1st lien holder can foreclose on the property, wiping out the borrower's equity and that of the 2nd position lien holder. This would enable the 1st position note holder to acquire the $100,000 property for the $80,000 originally invested (less the payments already received).

WHO NEEDS THE BANK?

What if the borrower damages the property or strips the home before vacating? Lenders on a property are named on the insurance policy as "also insured." If the property is damaged, a vandalism claim can be filed against the borrower's insurance policy and the property would be restored to its original condition for the cost of the deductible on the policy.

This rarely happens if borrowers are treated fairly. In over a decade of private lending, I've never had to file an insurance claim to restore a damaged property, but I've had to restore plenty of rentals when the tenants moved out! I felt it was important to share how the worst case scenarios would be resolved if they should occur. What other investment can you think of where the worst case scenario pays *more* than the best case scenario?

The secret to a long and lasting relationship with the borrower is a large down payment and a monthly payment that's less than the borrower would pay in rent. Everyone will experience an event (car accident, illness, etc.) in their lifetime that puts an unexpected strain on their finances.

If the borrower's monthly payment to *you* is less than they'd pay to rent the home across the street, it makes no sense for them to move. Besides losing their sizable down payment, they'd also have to pay moving expenses, fees to establish utility services, and would pay more to *rent* than they currently pay to *own*. When renting costs more than owning, borrowers will almost always find a way to pay!

5

What Documentation Is Needed?

"Memory is the thing you forget with."
- Alexander Chase

WHO NEEDS THE BANK?

The paperwork required for private loans is quite simple compared to the inch-thick pile of papers required for most bank loans. There are two documents required for private loans; a Promissory Note and either a Deed of Trust or Mortgage (depending on the State in which you live).

The Promissory Note is the borrower's promise to repay the loan and the Deed of Trust or Mortgage is the security instrument that secures the borrower's promise by pledging the property as collateral.

The promissory note is usually not recorded as it contains the terms and conditions of the loan that many borrowers wish to keep private. The Deed of Trust is signed in the presence of a Notary Public who is authorized by the State to attest to the authenticity of the signatures with an official seal of acknowledgement issued by the State.

After being signed by the borrower, the Deed of Trust or Mortgage is recorded by the County Recorder to inform the public that the debt exists and must be repaid before the property can be sold. Recording the document at the County Recorder's office places a time stamp on the document that establishes the priority in which the loan is repaid in the event more than one lien exists on the property.

The signed Promissory Note is the financial instrument used to document the debt and make the Note enforceable. This is a very important document that should be locked in a fireproof safe or held in a safe deposit box.

CHAPTER 5 – WHAT DOCUMENTATION IS NEEDED?

A Promissory Note is typically held by the Payee (person who is owed the money) but they can be bought and sold at any time during the term of the loan. When the debt has been fully repaid, the holder of the note must cancel the Note and return it to the Maker who borrowed the money.

The market for Promissory Notes has increased sharply in recent years as more and more individuals seek higher returns by offering loans to the millions of homebuyers turned down by banks. Borrowers usually make a large down payment to demonstrate their ability to make future payments to the seller carrying the financing.

Promissory Notes should contain this information:
1) Name and address of borrower(s) and lender(s)
2) Property address or description of the collateral
3) Original amount of the loan (in US dollars)
4) Term in months the buyer has to repay the loan
5) Annual interest rate (check State usury laws)
6) Interest start date and maturity date of the loan
7) Payment amount, 1st payment date and frequency
8) Payment type (interest only, amortized, paid at end)
9) Payment due date and penalty for late payments
10) Origination fee, points, or discount charged upfront
11) Prepayment penalty (if applicable) for early payoff
12) Due on sale clause if sold before loan is repaid
13) Escrow account for property tax and insurance
14) Balloon payment date and late fee per day if unpaid

WHO NEEDS THE BANK?

Be sure to read the documents that the closing attorney or escrow officer provides prior to signing them! An attorney typically prepares a draft document and then their assistants input the terms and conditions. These people are interrupted regularly and are often in a hurry, especially at the end of the month. They are human and make mistakes just like we all do.

Almost any mistake can be corrected if you catch it and make changes to the original instruments. My friend, Walter Wofford in Jackson, Mississippi, shared this checklist of things you'll want to verify to ensure that the information on the Note and Deed of Trust (or Mortgage) is accurate:

1) All information is filled in with no blanks
2) Legal description & address of property are correct
3) The dates on the Note are correct
4) Loan amount is correct (in words and numbers)
5) Interest rate is correct (in words and numbers)
6) Monthly payment is correct (in words and numbers)
7) First payment, due date & maturity date are correct
8) Late payment fee and grace period are correct
9) Name and address of borrower(s) is correct
10) Name and address of lender(s) is correct
11) Signatures on Note and Deed of Trust match

Reviewing these documents can be a bit confusing if you're not aware of some of the nuances of legal documents. The borrower may be referred to as Borrower, Payor, Grantor, Mortgagor, or Trustor. Titles that end with "or" usually refer to the person pledging the collateral (receiving the loan) and titles that end in "ee" refer to the person or entity receiving the collateral (lending the money).

CHAPTER 5 – WHAT DOCUMENTATION IS NEEDED?

A lender may be referred to as Lender, Payee, Grantee, or Mortgagee. In states with non-judicial foreclosures, the Beneficiary to a Deed of Trust is the Trustee to whom title is legally conveyed subject to the terms of the trust. This person acts as the referee of the transaction in the absence of a judge who would perform this duty in states that require a judicial foreclosure process.

The Promissory Note is usually not recorded and thus the original document should be delivered to the lender at closing or immediately after being signed by the borrower. A copy should be given to the borrower and the closing attorney for their files.

Be sure that the Deed of Trust or Mortgage will be returned to your address after being recorded by the County Recorder's office to avoid delays in getting the original back. It will be low in priority after everyone has been paid on the transaction!

WHO NEEDS THE BANK?

6

Aren't Banks "Safe" Investments?

"The more a person seeks security, the more that person gives up control over their life."

— Robert Kiyosaki

WHO NEEDS THE BANK?

Many Americans have grown up with the belief that banks are the "safest" place to keep their hard-earned savings. Every time we walk into a bank and see the FDIC logo on the door, we're reminded that our money is insured by the Federal Deposit Insurance Corporation.

According to the Federal Deposit Insurance Corporation website (www.FDIC.gov), the stated goal of the FDIC is "to preserve and promote public confidence in the U.S. financial system by insuring deposits in banks and thrift institutions for at least $250,000.00 by identifying, monitoring and addressing risks to the deposit insurance funds; and by limiting the effect on the economy."

Having your retirement nest egg insured by a government agency sounds great until you do a little digging and find out exactly how secure your finances really are. In 2018, more than $12 Trillion dollars in deposits was held in U.S. banks but the balance held in the Federal Deposit Insurance Corporation fund was only $75 Billion dollars.

How "safe" do you feel knowing that the FDIC insurance fund backing your life savings has reserves of just 6/10ths of one percent of the money it is meant to protect? To put this in perspective, the FDIC insurance fund has $6.25 for every $1,000.00 invested in U.S. banks.

The amount held in the FDIC insurance fund may seem very low, but when it was hit hard during the 2008 financial crisis, the FDIC was able to protect bank deposits through hundreds of bank failures.

CHAPTER 6 – AREN'T BANKS "SAFE" INVESTMENTS?

Banks are also highly leveraged due to *fractional reserve banking*, which provides banks with the leverage to lend out more than the *fraction* they're required to hold in reserves.

A bank's *capital* is the difference between their assets (cash, securities, and interest-earning loans) and their liabilities (debts owed on loans). Regulators monitor the ratio of outstanding loans to the amount the bank has in capital to establish a *"leverage ratio."*

The bank's leverage ratio limits the amount they can borrow in relation to their assets. Generally, a ratio of 4% is considered to be healthy, which means for every $1,000 a bank lends, they are required to have $40 in assets.

Due to this leverage, if property values decline, the bank's "assets" drop sharply. The debt owed to the bank's depositors and the Federal Reserve remains unchanged, thus ALL of the loss in value is subtracted from the bank's equity portion. If property values fall by 4%, all of the bank's equity would be wiped out and they would be required to invest additional capital to return to the 4% ratio.

If property values fall by more than 4% and the bank is unable to raise additional capital, the value of the bank's assets would be less than their liabilities and the bank would be deemed *insolvent*. When this occurs, the bank and all of its assets are seized by the government and placed into receivership. Leverage can produce great profits in rising markets but can have a vicious bite during market corrections! More than 500 banks failed between 2008 and 2015.

WHO NEEDS THE BANK?

The graph in *Table 6-1 Federal Reserve Home Price Index* shows that from 1975 to 2018, the average home price in the United States rose from $59,770 to $413,880, an increase of 692 percent! During this 43-year period, the housing market experienced only one major downturn, but it was catastrophic!

Table 6-1 - Federal Reserve Home Price Index

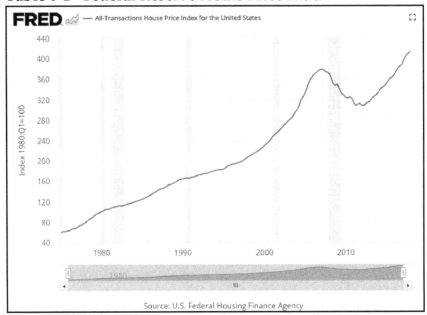

Home prices generally appreciate over time as the cost of labor and materials to build them increases. We rarely experience the massive declines that occurred from 2007 to 2012 during the Great Recession. Prior to that, the last major US banking system failure occurred in 1929 when the country was in the midst of the Great Depression. Most people would be happy with 78 years of profitability for every 5 years of loss, but when major people's lives are destroyed when it happens.

CHAPTER 6 – AREN'T BANKS "SAFE" INVESTMENTS?

If banks are allowed to lend 25 times more than the 4% they have in capital, then 96% of the money on every loan originated is created out of "thin air" by the Federal Reserve. For example, if a borrower obtains a home loan for $100,000, then $96,000 would come from the Federal Reserve and only $4,000 would come from funds the bank holds.

From 2007-2016, the interest rate that banks paid to the Federal Reserve was ¼ of one percent, but the interest rate banks charged consumers for home loans was between 3% and 4%. This represents a markup of 1,200% to 1,600% on money they never had in the first place!

With profits out of the stratosphere, one would think banks could pay retirees more than a fraction of one percent per year on their life's savings. Over time, inflation will push the cost of goods and services higher at a much faster rate than the interest income received from banks.

As the things we purchase become more expensive, the buying power of our money erodes accordingly. It seems that the investment we grew up believing was the "safest" is the surest way to LOSE!

WHO NEEDS THE BANK?

7

How Do Notes Compare to Banks?

"The U.S. government is the biggest debtor in the world, and those depending on it to take care of them will only become poorer."

- *Robert Kiyosaki*

WHO NEEDS THE BANK?

Chapter 6 illustrated the small percentage of capital banks invest in loans. In this chapter, we'll evaluate the amount borrowers are required to invest in the loan programs offered by banks.

Like banks, many of the borrowers approved for loans have little or no "skin" in the game. *Table 7-1 - Loan Comparison* provides a comparison to demonstrate the risk associated with different types of loans funded by mainstream banks.

Table 7-1 – Loan Comparison

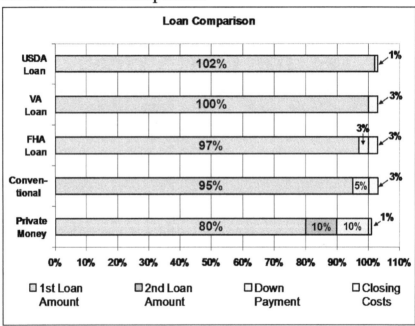

USDA Loans - The U.S. Department of Agriculture (the same people who put the stamp on your steak) offers loans up to 102% of the appraised value on rural properties. Assuming

CHAPTER 7 – HOW DO NOTES COMPARE TO BANKS?

closing costs of 3%, borrowers need only 1% of the purchase price to close and often ask the home sellers to pay them.

VA Loans - The Department of Veteran's Affairs (VA) is also in the mortgage business, offering loans up to 100% of appraised value to the veterans who serve or have served our country in the military. Many borrowers still have a hard time coming up with 3% for the closing costs and ask the home sellers to pay the fees for them.

FHA Loans - Prior to the Great Recession, the Federal Housing Administration offered loans with only 3.0% down. With so little "skin" in the game, many FHA loans failed, so to fix the problem, the government increased the minimum down payment to 3.5% (no kidding). FHA loans allow lower credit scores and many buyers are able to obtain grants for their down payment. FHA borrowers often ask home sellers to pay their closing costs, leaving them with little "skin" invested.

Conventional Loans - Conventional loans typically require the largest down payment of the programs offered by mainstream banks. The minimum down payment is typically 5% but the credit requirements are generally more stringent than other loan programs. Although these borrowers put more down and tend to have higher credit scores, they often ask home sellers to pay their closing costs.

Private Money Loans - As illustrated in *Table 7-1 – Loan Comparison*, the private money loan is by far the most *secure* loan because of the loan-to-value ratio (80% of appraised value in this example). We require a minimum down payment of at

WHO NEEDS THE BANK?

least 10% so the borrowers have more "skin" in the game than is required on any bank loan.

These 1st position loans are made even more secure by the 2nd position loan behind them. If the borrower stops paying, both the borrower's down payment and the 2nd position loan would be lost before any interest or principal is lost on the 1st position loan. Borrowers also pay their own closing costs, which further increases their "skin" in the game. Borrowers pay much lower closing costs on private loans when banks aren't involved in the process.

Table 7.2 – Negative Interest Rates

The Matrix: Race to Negative Bond Yields													
Country	1 Yr.	2 Yr.	3 Yr.	4 Yr.	5 Yr.	6 Yr.	7 Yr.	8 Yr.	9 Yr.	10 Yr.	15 Yr.	20 Yr.	30 Yr.
Switzerland	-0.87	-0.90	-0.94	-0.90	-0.87	-0.78	-0.73	-0.61	-0.51	-0.05	-0.19	-0.07	0.08
Japan	-0.26	-0.24	-0.24	-0.25	-0.24	-0.24	-0.24	-0.22	-0.18	-0.13	0.01	0.22	0.30
Germany	-0.53	-0.55	-0.56	-0.51	-0.42	-0.38	-0.31	-0.23	-0.10	0.03	0.13	0.36	0.63
Austria	-0.50	-0.50	-0.44	-0.42	-0.39	-0.22	-0.16	-0.07	0.09	0.23	0.31	0.81	1.07
Netherlands		-0.49	-0.46	-0.42	-0.25	-0.23	-0.11	-0.01	0.13	0.25			0.75
Belgium	-0.51	-0.49	-0.46	-0.41	-0.35	-0.25	-0.14	0.12	0.28	0.43	0.81	0.90	1.34
Finland	-0.52	-0.48	-0.45	-0.33	-0.28	-0.12	-0.06	0.03	0.17	0.34	0.58		0.78
France		-0.50	-0.44	-0.40	-0.33	-0.20	-0.14	-0.03	0.09	0.25	0.39	0.75	1.04	1.22
Sweden	-0.50	-0.63		-0.52	-0.33		-0.06			0.30		1.06	
Denmark		-0.40			-0.17	0.31				0.29			0.74
Ireland	-0.18		-0.31	-0.15	-0.07	0.12	0.30	0.50	0.66	0.73	1.09		1.59
Italy	-0.15	-0.06	-0.04	0.19	0.40	0.50	0.79	1.00	1.21	1.38	1.71	2.04	2.43
Spain	-0.16	-0.10	0.00	0.24	0.45	0.49	0.73	1.09	1.24	1.42	1.82		2.57
United States	0.57	0.76	0.91		1.21		1.49			1.68			2.48

Interest rates on loans funded by banks are much higher than they were during the Great Recession, but there's downward pressure on the interest banks pay on deposits. As illustrated in the chart in *Table 7.2 – Negative Interest Rates*

CHAPTER 7 – HOW DO NOTES COMPARE TO BANKS?

published by Pension Partners in 2016, many European banks no longer pay interest to depositors on bonds and actually *charge* depositors for the privilege of holding their money!

American banks reportedly paid an average of 0.57% on 1-year bonds, but from 2007 to 2018 many mainstream banks in the United States paid 0.2% interest or less to their depositors. If you shop around for a "good" bank paying 0.2% interest per year, your $100,000.00 investment would net $200.00 per year, which is only $16.67 per month!

How will your retirement lifestyle be affected if the income on $100,000.00 won't even buy one cup of Starbucks coffee each week? If you're married, you'll either have to share with your spouse or take turns with your own coffee every other week! This is not the case with notes!

WHO NEEDS THE BANK?

8

Should Baby Boomers Buy Notes?

"To get rich, you have to be making money while you're asleep."

- David Bailey

WHO NEEDS THE BANK?

During the 19 years after World War II, 80 million babies were born in the United States. This period of history was dubbed the "baby boom" and those born between 1946 and 1964 became know as the Baby Boom generation.

At the time, boomers represented 40% of the U.S. population and disrupted the American way of life at every turn. They overcrowded inner-city schools, creating the need for suburbs and two automobiles per household. As they aged, boomers traded their banana seat bicycles for muscle cars, grew out their hair, listened to rock and roll music, and demanded the right to vote at the age of 18.

As their suburban families grew and Mary Tyler Moore appeared on TV wearing pants, boomers challenged the role of women as homemakers, which led to the creation of TV dinners, packaged snacks, and fast food. With two incomes, the standard of living in America increased sharply. For the first time, families had disposable income to purchase refrigerators, washing machines, vacuum cleaners, electric mixers, microwave ovens, and other products that could save time and make their lives easier.

The most popular product by far was the television, which was in only 7,000 homes in 1946, but had invaded 50 million households by 1960. During decades of economic prosperity, TV ads promoted new products and boomers began using credit cards to purchase cars, clothes, pet rocks, and hula hoops. Television watching became a nightly activity as advertisers redefined the American lifestyle.

CHAPTER 8 – SHOULD BABY BOOMERS BUY NOTES?

Due to interstate highways, air conditioning, computers, and other technological advances, Americans suddenly had the freedom to change jobs and relocate to Sunbelt states that were previously thought to be too hot and humid. This mobility ended the idea of life-long employment and corporate pensions were replaced with IRAs and 401(k) plans. These investment vehicles placed the responsibility of saving for retirement on *individuals* rather than companies, but many boomers didn't start early enough or save enough to live for decades after retirement.

The parents of baby boomers retired at 65 and lived 5 to 7 years after retirement but due to advances in medicine, active boomers who refuse to age are living 10 to 25 years longer than their parents. This presents a problem because when baby boomers were working, there were *six* workers per retiree. By the time all the baby boomers retire, the ratio will be *three* workers for each retired baby boomer.

With ever-increasing health care costs and tens of millions of people living much longer than expected, there's legitimate concern that the Social Security payments boomers have made since their teens will fall drastically short of providing the monthly income and health-related services required to combat cancer, heart disease, diabetes, and dementia.

When the parents of baby boomers retired in the 1980s, bank interest rates were as high as 18%, but by 2007 annual interest rates had fallen to 0.2%, which isn't enough income to live on, even with more savings.

WHO NEEDS THE BANK?

More and more baby boomers are working into their 70s because they lost a substantial portion of their net worth in the mortgage meltdown and the stock market crash that followed. More than half of baby boomers still have a monthly mortgage payment and are unable to make ends meet without at least some income from a job.

Many people don't start saving for retirement until they reach their 50s. Few baby boomers anticipated that the recession and slow recovery afterward would thwart their ability to save during what they thought would be the best decade of their career. To make matters worse, few were able to downsize when home values were low because they owed more on their home than it was worth.

By the time home values increased and they were no longer upside-down, the cost of the homes boomers hoped to purchase also increased and were more than they could afford. Aging boomers who are caught in this trap are moving their children and grandchildren in with them to share the cost of taxes, utilities, insurance, and HOA fees. The 2000 Census reported that 3.9 million American households had three generations or more living together and 78,000 households had four generations under one roof. The number of multi-generational households in the U.S. hasn't been this high since the early 50s and has increased by nearly 60 percent since 2000.

If boomers find themselves trapped in their homes, they can offset their mortgage payment with the income from notes purchased with the equity from a reverse mortgage. More can be found about reverse mortgages in Chapter 17.

9

Are Notes Better Than Stocks?

"One of the funny things about the stock market is that every time one person buys, another sells, and both think they are astute.

- William Feather

WHO NEEDS THE BANK?

In 2011, the leading edge of the baby boomers began to turn 65 years old. As retirement approaches, many people feverishly plow as much as they can into the stock market in hopes of reaping a large enough return to compensate for their inability to save during the first five decades of their lives.

Between 2011 and 2029, more than 10,000 baby boomers in the United States will turn 65 years old *every single day!* That's 300,000 people a month and 3.6 million people each year for 19 years! As these boomers retire, two things happen:

1) They stop putting money *into* the stock market
2) They start taking money *out of* the stock market

In a free market economy, the value of a commodity is a function of supply and demand. How will the stock market be affected as thousands of people every day stop *buying* stocks, and instead begin *selling* their shares to cover monthly living expenses? Are the children and grandchildren of the boomers investing enough money in the stock market to make up the difference? I don't think so!

With fewer buyers and more sellers each day, high school economics tells us that the supply of stocks will increase as demand for shares decreases. Who will buy the stocks being sold and *at what price?* Do you really want to roll the dice in the Wall Street casino with your ability to retire on the line?

When you're younger and retirement is decades away, you can stomach the volatility of the stock market because you don't need the money any time soon. That changes when you

CHAPTER 9 – ARE NOTES BETTER THAN STOCKS?

need to withdraw cash to pay your living expenses. For most retirees, investing in the stock market is no longer an option because they can't replace potential losses with income.

As they settle into retirement, many people are shocked at how fast they burn through their money. It's usually not late night binge-buying on home shopping channels that causes a problem. The increased spending often takes place during the 10 to 12 hours each day that were previously spent commuting to and working at their jobs.

Instead of earning income during most of their day, retirees suddenly have the entire day to spend on leisure activities, which usually require money. Lower income and higher expenses can create a huge budget deficit that must be dealt with immediately. Many retirees take part-time jobs or volunteer at charities so they won't be tempted to spend money throughout the day.

Unfortunately, some people turn to the stock market to solve their budget deficits. This may work great during times when the market is rising, but corrections can be devastating! Because they're gambling with their life's savings, many retirees panic when the market corrects and sell their investments for much less than they paid. Their attempt to preserve capital often negates any gains they may have realized and they end up with less than they initially invested.

The stock market is usually not a good idea for those on a fixed income because the income is not as predictable as the bills that arrive like clockwork every month. Investments that offer predictable payments often offer a substantially lower return than you could receive with real estate notes. There's an abundance of data to demonstrate the stock market has been overvalued for decades. The chart presented in *Table 9-1 – Market Cap to GDP* was created by William Baldwin and appeared in Forbes magazine in July, 2018.

Table 9-1 – Market Cap to GDP

In 1975, you could purchase all of the publicly traded stocks in the U.S. for a sum equal to 40% of that year's gross domestic product. Today, the cost per dollar of GDP would be four times higher.

How much do you really know about the companies you invest in on the stock market? Why invest in something you don't understand when you can invest in notes secured by real estate that you can drive by in your local community?

10

Are Notes Better Than Rentals?

"The debt on the apartment houses I own is good debt only as long as there are tenants to pay my mortgages. If tenants stop paying their rent, my good debt turns into bad debt."

— *Robert Kiyosaki*

WHO NEEDS THE BANK?

The most common way to invest in real estate is to own rental property. I'm certain that you've heard horror stories from landlords who deal with the "tenant and toilet" issues associated with their rental properties.

There are also times when tenants move out and rental properties sit vacant or require major repairs. During these times, the property owner not only earns no income but may be required to pay thousands of dollars for repairs. It's much better to be a *lender* on the property than a janitor who isn't compensated for cleaning other people's dirt!

What if you could earn 5 to 50 times more than the interest at the bank, avoid the daily volatility of the stock market, and the hassles of owning rental properties? Over the past decade, I've taught thousands of retirees, investors and burned-out property owners how to become "lienlords" instead of landlords.

Providing loans to qualified borrowers creates a unique opportunity to obtain the high returns of real estate investments without the hassles of ownership. With notes you receive "mailbox money" every month without the drama, expenses, or phone calls that come with rental properties.

Table 10.1 – Monthly Rental Property Expenses shows the typical expenses on a rental property producing gross monthly rent of $1,000. Although vacancy and major repairs don't occur on a consistent basis, funds should be set aside monthly to create adequate reserves for repairs when inevitable events occur (usually when you're on the way out of town).

CHAPTER 10 – ARE NOTES BETTER THAN RENTALS?

Table 10.1 – Monthly Rental Property Expenses

EXPENSE	COST/ MONTH
Property Management (10%)	$100
Repairs & Maintenance	$100
Property Tax	$150
Hazard Insurance	$50
Vacancy (5%)	$50
TOTAL	$450

Assuming the management, repair, taxes, insurance, and vacancy expenses listed above, a landlord could expect to pay about $450 of their $1,000 gross monthly rent in expenses. That leaves just $550 to pay the mortgage or retain as profit if the property is owned without a loan.

To calculate the annual rate of return that the $550 monthly income represents, we'd need to know the value of the property. Assuming that the property could be sold for $150,000 we'd multiply the $550 net monthly rent by 12 to find the net income for the year ($550 x 12 = $6,600) and then divide the net annual income by the property value to calculate the rate of return on the capital invested in the property ($6,600 / $150,000 = 4.4%).

A yield of 4.4% is much better than banks pay, but time and effort must be exerted to achieve that return. Even when rental properties are professionally managed, property owners must oversee them to maintain this rate of return. If instead, the landlord sold the property for $160,000, received a $20,000

WHO NEEDS THE BANK?

down payment, and carried a loan of $140,000 at 5% interest for 30 years, they'd receive payments of $751.55.

Why collect $1,000 and pay out $450 in bills every month when you can receive an automatic deposit from the note servicing company for $201.55 more and you never get a phone call? If you invest the $20,000 down payment in another 30-year note at 5%, you'd receive an additional payment of $107.36, bringing the monthly difference to $308.91.

In this scenario, the same set of keys is handed off but instead of receiving a $1,000 security deposit, the investor gets a cashier's check for $20,000. The landlord also hands off the $450 in monthly expenses, future vacancies, and the hassles of dealing with tenants! The effort required by a note holder involves simply walking to the mailbox once a month or logging into their online account to verify that the payment has been received from the servicing company!

Besides producing more income with less hassle, notes offer less risk than property ownership. If someone is injured on the premises, they'll sue the landlord who owns the property, not the lender who funded the note. Even if the landlord loses a lawsuit, the lender's position is secure because they have a recorded lien in 1st position that is paid all of the principal and interest owed before junior liens are paid a cent.

Renters are far less likely to treat a property with the same respect an owner does. For this reason, many people want nothing to do with renters or the hassles of owning rental property, and I'm one of them! I'll take a $20,000 cashier's check over a $1,000 security deposit every time!

11

How Do I Compare Investments?

"Leave no stone unturned to help your clients realize maximum profits from their investment."
— *Arthur C. Nielsen*

WHO NEEDS THE BANK?

Money invested in a bank at 0.2% would take 5 years to earn 1% and 25 years to earn 5%. In contrast, a private loan might pay 5% in a single year, which would produce monthly income 25 times higher than the interest paid by a bank. To quickly realize the difference between investments, calculate what you could buy with the interest. Earning 5% instead of 0.2% would be the equivalent of getting twenty-five bags of groceries for the same price you currently pay for just one!

This example demonstrates the impact note investing can have on your lifestyle. If you could afford one vacation per year on the 0.2% interest paid by a bank, then you could take twenty-five vacations with the income from a 5% note! Just think of the difference a higher yield could make on your lifestyle over time. Albert Einstein called compound interest the eighth wonder of the world, and observed, "He who understands interest, *earns* it and he who doesn't, *pays* it."

The Rule of 72 is an easy way to quantify the difference between investments. To determine how long it takes for an investment to double in value, simply divide 72 by the interest rate (no decimals). As illustrated in *Table 11-1 – The Rule of 72*, an investment of $10,000.00 earning 3% would take 24 years to double (72/ 3 = 24) and would double again in 24 years.

If you invest the same $10,000.00 at 6%, it would take only 12 years to double (72/ 6 = 12), and the value would double *four times* in 48 years instead of twice. Simple math would suggest that since 6% is twice as much as 3% the total would be twice as much, but the return is four times greater because the balance was doubled four times instead of twice.

CHAPTER 11 – HOW DO I COMPARE INVESTMENTS?

If the $10,000.00 was invested at 12%, it would double every 6 years (72/ 12 = 6) and your $10,000.00 investment would double *eight times* over the same 48 year period!

Table 11-1 – The Rule of 72

RULE OF 72			
YEARS	**3%**	**6%**	**12%**
NOW	$10,000	$10,000	$10,000
6			$20,000
12		$20,000	$40,000
18			$80,000
24	$20,000	$40,000	$160,000
30			$320,000
36		$80,000	$640,000
42			$1,280,000
48	$40,000	$160,000	$2,560,000

After 48 years, the value of your $10,000 investment would be $2,560,000 if invested at 12% instead of the $40,000 you'd earn at 3% interest or the $160,000 that would be achieved at 6% interest.

Money invested in a bank paying 0.2% annual interest would take *360 years* to double! That's 100 years longer than the United States has been a country! It would take 14 generations for your family to see your $10,000 investment double to $20,000! Do you think grocery prices will increase over the next 360 years? You can't afford to invest your money in the bank or anywhere else at such a low rate of return!

Interest rates are often a function of *risk*. High risk investments typically offer a higher return to entice investors to accept the higher level of risk. In contrast, low risk investments appeal to more people and thus create a much higher demand. These investments typically offer a lower rate of return because of the security they offer and the demand they generate from investors.

Because few people are aware that they can invest in real estate notes, the *demand* for private money loans is much higher than supply of people who finance them. This creates a market imbalance which drives the rate of return higher without proportionately increasing the risk.

All investments have some element of risk, no matter how "safe" they may seem. The rate of return you select should be determined by your age, your tolerance for risk, and whether you have the time and ability to replace the money invested.

Retired people often can't afford to lose their investment capital because they don't have the ability to replace it. Low risk typically coincides with a low return but because of the mismatch between supply and demand, real estate notes pay much higher yields than banks.

12

Are Notes Better Investments?

"Surplus wealth is a sacred trust which its possessor is bound to administer in his lifetime for the good of the community."

- Andrew Carnegie

WHO NEEDS THE BANK?

I invest in real estate notes because they produce consistent income for decades without the volatility of the stock market. The rate of return is exponentially higher than the interest offered by banks, and by owning the *paper* instead of the *property* I avoid the liability and hassles of being a landlord. I also avoid paying property managers, property tax, hazard insurance, repair bills, maintenance expenses, and the "vacancy thief" when the property is not rented.

It's much easier to understand your local real estate market than the complexities of other investments. With notes, I can assess the condition of the home being pledged as collateral, analyze the neighborhood in which it's located, check the value of the property on several online valuation websites, and I can even meet the borrowers before I lend the money! Other investments don't offer the ease and level of understanding you get by funding notes in your local market.

Many retirees are on fixed incomes and no longer have the ability to work. At this stage of life, maintaining the value of your assets is more important than earning a high return. I don't think retired people should lend more than 80% of a property's value or invest in anything but 1st position notes.

Unfortunately, bad things happen to good people and everyone can expect to die at some point. If an unexpected event causes the borrower to default on the loan, the 2nd lien holder would have to foreclose on the borrower to protect their position. Failure to do so would cause their lien to be wiped out if the 1st lien holder foreclosed.

CHAPTER 13 – HOW DO I QUALIFY THE BORROWER?

The *position* of a note is the priority in which it is repaid in the event of a default. 2nd position liens can produce lucrative returns but are much riskier because if the borrower defaults, the 2nd position lien holder isn't paid until the lien holder in 1st position has been paid their principal and interest.

The public school system does little to educate children about managing their finances and teaches nothing about note investing. Because so few people know about notes, it's been the best-kept secret of savvy investors for centuries!

An added benefit of notes is that they become more secure as you age. With each monthly payment, the amount you're owed *decreases* slightly but appreciation usually causes the value of the property held as collateral to *increase.* This makes your note investment more secure over time. As the borrower accumulates equity each month through principal reduction and market appreciation, the already low risk of default becomes even less likely.

Home values in the United States have averaged annual appreciation of over 3% since World War II. The Rule of 72 tells us that at 3% appreciation, the value of a home will double in 24 years (72/3 = 24). *Table 12-1 – Loan to Value Over Time* shows how quickly the loan-to-value ratio (LTV) decreases.

If you held a 30-year note earning 5% interest and the property appreciated by 3% per year, the loan-to-value ratio would fall from 80% in the first year to 60% by the 6th year. By the 10th year of the loan, the balance would represent less than half of the property's value, significantly reducing your risk!

Table 12-1 - Loan to Value Over Time

Year	Loan Balance	Market Value	Loan to Value
Now	$80,000	$100,000	80.0%
1	$78,820	$103,000	76.5%
2	$77,579	$106,090	73.1%
3	$76,275	$109,273	69.8%
4	$74,904	$112,551	66.6%
5	$73,463	$115,927	63.4%
6	$71,948	$119,405	60.3%
7	$70,356	$122,987	57.2%
8	$68,682	$126,677	54.2%
9	$66,923	$130,477	51.3%
10	$65,074	$134,392	48.4%
11	$63,130	$138,423	45.6%
12	$61,086	$142,576	42.8%
13	$58,938	$146,853	40.1%
14	$56,680	$151,259	37.5%
15	$54,307	$155,797	34.9%
16	$51,812	$160,471	32.3%
17	$49,190	$165,285	29.8%
18	$46,433	$170,243	27.3%
19	$43,536	$175,351	24.8%
20	$40,490	$180,611	22.4%
21	$37,288	$186,029	20.0%
22	$33,923	$191,610	17.7%
23	$30,385	$197,359	15.4%
24	$26,666	$203,279	13.1%
25	$22,757	$209,378	10.9%
26	$18,648	$215,659	8.6%
27	$14,329	$222,129	6.5%
28	$9,789	$228,793	4.3%
29	$5,017	$235,657	2.1%
30	$0	$242,726	0.0%

13

How Do I Qualify The Borrower?

"In action a great heart is the chief qualification; in work, a great head."

- Arthur Schopenhauer

WHO NEEDS THE BANK?

Don't spend much time worrying about how to qualify the borrower because this is something that you shouldn't be doing. Leave the qualification process to a professional Mortgage Loan Originator (MLO) licensed in the state where the property is located.

The MLO will provide the documentation necessary to comply with state and federal laws and will have the borrower complete and sign a mortgage application that provides information about their income, assets, liabilities, and debt. The borrower will be asked to provide recent pay stubs, bank statements, mortgage statements, income tax returns, and other documentation necessary to verify the information on their application. The best thing you can do is get out of the way and let the licensed lender do their job!

The MLO will also access the borrower's credit history, which is also known as their *FICO Score.* Fair, Isaac, and Company (FICO) first introduced their credit scoring model in 1989 which takes various factors of a person's financial history into account that help to predict the likelihood of default. The score is a proprietary calculation derived from the borrower's payment history, debt burden, credit history, types of credit used, and recent credit searches.

When determining whether or not to approve borrowers for a loan, banks often evaluate five aspects of the borrower's credit, all of which ironically begin with the letter C. The five C's of credit include: *character, capacity, capital, collateral, and conditions.* The five criteria are summarized as follows:

CHAPTER 13 – HOW DO I QUALIFY THE BORROWER?

Character refers to a borrower's past credit history. The credit report provides a loan-by-loan breakdown of the borrower's payment history on all the loans they've obtained in their lifetime. This report lists the amount borrowed, the number of payments made, and the timeliness in which the payments were received.

Capacity refers to a borrower's ability to repay their outstanding loans. The Dodd-Frank Wall Street Reform and Consumer Protection Act of 2010 made lenders accountable if they provide loans to borrowers who have more than 43% of their gross income going toward the payment of debt. Capacity can also be affected if borrowers are employed in unstable jobs or have a sporadic employment history.

Capital refers to the net worth of the borrower. Net worth can be determined by subtracting the borrower's total liabilities (debt) from their total assets. Banks like to see free and clear assets that could be sold if an emergency arises. Borrowers with a lot of assets demonstrate that they have the ability to save and be financially responsible.

Collateral refers to the value of the property on which you place a lien. On a mortgage, the collateral is the home and on a vehicle loan, the collateral is the car. Holding an asset as collateral gives lenders recourse to take ownership of the asset if the loan is not repaid as promised.

Conditions refer to external factors such as the economy. If a major employer in the area is closing down a factory or the housing market is very soft, lenders may tighten their lending

WHO NEEDS THE BANK?

standards until they can get a sense of how the local economy will be affected by the change.

Below is a checklist of documents that would typically be required by a licensed MLO:

- ☐ W-2s for the past two (2) years (all borrowers/all jobs)
- ☐ Pay stubs for the most recent month of employment (all borrowers/all jobs, 30 days minimum)
- ☐ Signed Federal income tax returns, with all schedules (if applicable), for the past two (2) years.
- ☐ Asset account statements for the past (2) months including checking, savings, money market accounts; and investment accounts for stocks and bonds.
- ☐ Most recent retirement account statement(s) for borrower's 401(k), pensions, and annuities
- ☐ Most current mortgage, tax, and insurance statements for all properties owned
- ☐ If renting, current landlord's name, address, and phone number or 12 consecutive months of cancelled rent checks.
- ☐ Current lease agreements for all rental properties
- ☐ Copies of separation or divorce decree, support order, and property settlement agreement, if applicable
- ☐ If using child support or alimony to qualify, a one (1) year history printout from the Domestic Relations Department
- ☐ Copy of driver's license, Social Security card, or passport. Copy of green card for resident aliens

CHAPTER 13 – HOW DO I QUALIFY THE BORROWER?

☐ Copy of fully-executed purchase agreement for the property being purchased

☐ Real estate listing agreement or purchase agreement if borrower is selling an existing home

Although all of this information is helpful in making lending decisions, don't expect to find credit history without blemishes. Bad things happen to good people every day, including job loss, divorce, car accidents, sickness, and death.

Many of these events are one-time occurrences that aren't within the borrower's control and are unlikely to reoccur in the future. The high cost of health care has plagued borrowers for years, but most major credit bureaus no longer penalize borrowers for medical debt they can't pay.

You may need to be flexible to accommodate borrowers who have good income but don't have a lot saved. Some borrowers have plenty of income and assets but can't seem to get their bills paid on time. To offset poor credit, you may consider requiring a larger down payment, charging an origination fee, requiring automated payments directly from their bank account, and imposing the maximum late fee.

For a down payment shortage, you can create an additional note for the difference and charge a higher rate of interest for assuming more risk. I'm usually willing to overlook blemishes on a borrower's credit report but I won't lend to people who are behind on other payments (other than

WHO NEEDS THE BANK?

medical debt). I have no interest in having to hunt down borrowers to be paid!

14

Will I Become A Bill Collector?

"An improving credit landscape means fewer loans are delinquent and fewer people are needed to service these loans.

- Kayla Tausche

WHO NEEDS THE BANK?

Loan servicing is another task that should be left to competent professionals who are licensed in the state where the property is located. A mortgage servicer is responsible for collecting the borrower's monthly payments, setting aside funds in an escrow account for property tax and insurance, making principal and interest payments to lien holders, preparing monthly statements, sending IRS 1099 forms to lenders and 1098 forms to borrowers to document interest earned and paid, pursuing delinquent payments and mailing notices if necessary.

Whew! That's a lot to take care of and well worth the servicing fee. The account setup and monthly servicing fees are usually paid by the borrower, so it's best to just get out of the way and let the servicer do their job!

The Fair Debt Collection Practices Act (FDCPA) is a federal law that limits the behavior and actions of debt collectors. There are also state laws which can add additional limits on who can contact consumers, the method by which they may be reached, and the hours of the day and number of times they may be called.

An age old question in lending is whether a borrower's *credit score* or *down payment* is more important. Banks seem to base their decisions on the borrower's credit score, but I rely more on the down payment, which reflects the borrower's "skin" in the game. A benefit of living through the 2008 financial crisis is that we now have the data to prove whether credit score or down payment is a better predictor of whether borrowers will default on their loans.

CHAPTER 14 – WILL I BECOME A BILL COLLECTOR?

The chart in *Table 14-1 – 7-Year Foreclosure Completion Rate* was published in 2013 by the Federal Housing Finance Agency to document the foreclosure rates of Fannie Mae and Freddie Mac loans originated between 1995 and 2008.

Table 14-1 – 7-Year Foreclosure Completion Rate

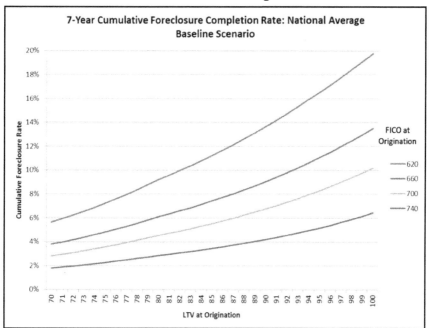

The loans foreclosed on during the 7-years of the Great Recession are categorized by the borrower's FICO score in ranges of 620 to 659, 660 to 699, 700 to 739, and 740 and above. The ranges are charted by the loan-to-value (LTV) ratio at the time the loans were originated to indicate how much the borrowers put down. At bottom left are the borrowers who put 30% down payment and obtained a loan for 70%. During the worst seven years since the Great Depression, less than 2% of borrowers with a 740 FICO score were foreclosed on.

WHO NEEDS THE BANK?

Even though their credit scores were 120 points lower, borrowers with a 620 FICO score fared nearly as well with just 5.66% failing over the 7-year period. That's a failure rate less than 1% per year during a disastrous time of economic turmoil. A 99% success rate in any business is amazing!

The right side of the chart tells a different story. Borrowers with little or no "skin" in the game didn't do nearly as well. During the same 7 year period, 6% of borrowers with a 740+ FICO score (very high) were foreclosed on and nearly 20% of those with a 620 FICO score defaulted.

The failure rate of borrowers with a 620 FICO score was three times higher than borrowers with a 740 score on both ends of the spectrum, but less than 6% of borrowers with a 30% down payment failed in *seven years* while nearly 20% with low or no down payment failed. A combination of good credit and large down payment would be ideal, but if I had to choose between the two, I'd go with a larger down payment!

We require a down payment of at least 10% of the purchase price. This requirement disqualifies a lot of people, but home ownership in not a *right!* Using someone's life savings is a privilege that should be reserved for those who've demonstrated the discipline to save for the down payment.

A brief published in August, 2012 by the Center for Responsible Lending estimated the number of years it would take middle-class workers in different occupations to save 10% for the down payment on a home. They assumed a median home price of $158,100, median household income of

CHAPTER 14 – WILL I BECOME A BILL COLLECTOR?

$50,046.00, and an annual savings rate of 2% dedicated toward the down payment. Their findings are presented in *Table 14-2 – Years to Save for a 10% Down Payment*.

Table 14-2 – Years to Save for a 10% Down Payment

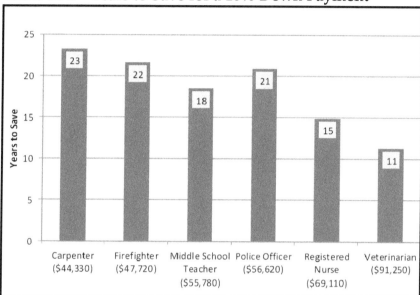

The analysis shows that it would take carpenters, fire fighters, and police officers over *twenty years* to accumulate a 10% down payment! Middle school teachers, registered nurses and veterinarians would have to save 2% of their income for over *ten years* to accumulate the 10% down payment.

Banks don't require 10% down because few people are disciplined enough to make it, but borrowers with a down payment of 10% or more are far less likely to default. A large down payment significantly lowers the odds that either you or the servicing company will become a bill collector!

WHO NEEDS THE BANK?

15

How Do I Set the Interest Rate?

"The charge that a bank makes for the use of its notes, the interest, is a continual and universal tax upon all members of the community."

— John Buchanan Robinson

WHO NEEDS THE BANK?

Bank interest rates are usually very competitive, but for borrowers who don't fit within the bank's guidelines, interest rates can vary widely between loans. Interest is directly correlated to the level of *risk* being assumed. Several factors should be considered, including the amount of the borrower's down payment, the length of time the money will be invested, the location, value, and condition of the collateral, the credit history of the borrower, etc. Due to variance in these factors, there is no set interest rate. Lenders must assess the risks of each investment and adjust the rate and terms accordingly.

For any deal to last, it must be good for all parties. The interest rate of a loan is no different. If an investor asks for a rate that is too high, their money will sit undeployed earning nothing or a very low rate of interest at the bank. Borrowers who are desperate enough to pay a high rate of interest will struggle to make the payments, increasing the likelihood of default. Unfortunately, some unscrupulous people lend with the intention of later foreclosing and reselling the property.

The rate of interest is written into the promissory note when the note is originated and cannot be changed. In order to set the interest, you must *originate* the note. To do that you must either own the property being financed or have a mortgage loan originator's license. You can purchase notes that someone else originated, but the terms of the loan cannot be altered.

Buyers who can't obtain bank financing must purchase properties from home sellers who are willing to act as a bank and provide "carry back" financing. If the home seller later

CHAPTER 15 – HOW DO I SET THE INTEREST RATE?

needs capital for another investment, they can sell the note and the payment stream that goes with it to another investor.

Those who buy notes often have other investment options available to them. If the interest rate is too low, the note may be difficult to sell. Notes with a low rate of return would likely have to be discounted and sold at a lower price to compete with other investment options paying higher returns.

Before buying a note, you should ensure that the loan was originated using a mortgage loan originator licensed in the state where the property is located. This ensures that the terms of the note are compliant with SAFE, RESPA, FDCPA, TILA, and Regulation Z legislation and local usury laws. A brief description of each is below:

SAFE Act – Secure and Fair Enforcement for Mortgage Licensing Act of 2008 was created to enhance consumer protection and reduce fraud by encouraging states to establish minimum standards for licensing mortgage loan originators.

RESPA – Real Estate Settlement Procedures Act is a federal law passed by congress in 1974 to eliminate the kickbacks and referral fees prevalent in the industry at the time and to enable consumers to become better shoppers for settlement services.

FDCPA – Fair Debt Collection Practices Act is a federal law that prohibits debt collectors from using abusive, unfair, or deceptive practices to collect payments from consumers. Some states require that you have a Mortgage Loan Originator's license to even speak with a borrower!

WHO NEEDS THE BANK?

TILA – Truth in Lending Act is a federal law passed in 1968 to ensure that lenders treat consumers fairly. Lenders are required to disclose all fees being charged to obtain loans so consumers are informed of the true cost of the credit being extended to them.

Regulation Z – Regulation Z is the portion of the Truth in Lending Act that protects consumers against misleading practices by lenders. All lenders are required to disclose the loan amount, interest rate, term, payment and all fees when advertising a loan, not just the monthly payment.

In addition to federal laws, each state has usury laws which limit the amount of interest that can be legally charged to consumers. If the loan paperwork was prepared by an attorney licensed in the state in which you do business, this will not be something you have to worry about. Title companies are typically owned by attorneys or have an attorney on staff to prepare loan documents that comply with state and federal laws.

These laws should not scare you or dissuade you from becoming a private lender. It's important to know that they exist, but rather than trying to become an expert on the laws that must be followed, simply use a licensed mortgage loan originator to qualify the borrower, a real estate attorney to draft the loan documents, and a licensed loan servicer to collect the payments and disburse funds.

To earn a fee for providing a loan, you must have a Mortgage Loan Originator's license, but providing borrowers

CHAPTER 15 – HOW DO I SET THE INTEREST RATE?

with uncompensated, general information about mortgages or lists of reputable lenders who make private loans is not generally considered to be an activity that requires a license. Check with an attorney in your state to be sure!

The information contained in this chapter is intended for educational purposes and should not be considered legal or business advice. Laws vary from state to state, change over time, and can sometimes vary in different situations. If you have questions about how any of the rules discussed in this chapter apply to you, it's best to hire a competent attorney who specializes in real estate law, is licensed in the state where you reside or wish to do business, and invests in notes themselves.

If you're selling a home and are thinking about carrying back the financing, there is a tax-saving strategy that you may wish to consider. If you've lived in your home for two of the past five years, the capital gain on the sale could be tax free, but you'll have to pay income tax on the interest you earn on the note each year. In this situation, it would be better from a tax perspective, to sell your home at a higher price and in return charge the buyer a lower rate of interest.

For a buyer purchasing a home with financing, it would be better to negotiate a lower price and a higher interest rate because mortgage interest is tax deductible (to a point) and can lower the amount owed in income tax. When the buyers wish to refinance the loan at a lower interest rate, they would have more equity in the home and the amount of their loan would be lower, making it easier to refinance.

WHO NEEDS THE BANK?

16

What If I'm Not Ready to Retire?

"Preparation for old age should begin not later than one's teens. A life which is empty of purpose until 65 will not suddenly become filled on retirement."

— Dwight L. Moody

WHO NEEDS THE BANK?

I use retirees in examples throughout this book because they've had more time to save than younger generations, but you don't have to be retired to own notes! Real estate notes are great investments for Coverdell Educational Savings Accounts, Health Savings Accounts, Roth IRAs, and Roth 401(k) plans, all of which provide tax-free returns! You can also purchase notes in self-directed 401(k) and Individual Retirement Accounts.

If you fund a 30-year note for $100,000 earning 6% interest, you'll receive payments of $599.55 every month for 30 years but you'll likely be paid off much sooner. The National Association of Realtors data in *Table 16-1 - Median Seller Tenure* was published by Keeping Current Matters in 2018. The data shows that between 1986 and 2016 home sellers averaged only 5 to 10 years in their homes before selling.

Table 16-1 – Median Seller Tenure

CHAPTER 16 – WHAT IF I'M NOT READY TO RETIRE?

If your note is paid off after five years, you'll receive 60 monthly payments totaling $35,973.00, but the buyer will still owe $93,054.36. The payments received in the first five years represent nearly 36% of your original investment, but less than 7% ($6,945.64) is applied toward the principal balance.

If your note is repaid in 10 years, you'll receive 120 monthly payments totaling $71,946.00 but the buyer will still owe $83,685.72. The payments received during the first ten years total nearly 72% of your original investment, but only 16.3% ($16,314.28) is applied toward the principal balance.

If payments are reinvested, a $100,000 investment will grow to $198,253.86 in 10 years, giving you nearly enough to buy *two* $100,000 notes, which doubles your monthly income! If those notes were paid off in 10 years (20 years from now) you'd have nearly enough to fund *four* $100,000 notes.

Table 16-2 – Notes Accumulated

TIME	# of NOTES	VALUE
NOW	1	$100,000
10 Years	2	$200,000
20 Years	4	$400,000
30 Years	8	$800,000
40 Years	16	$1,600,000
50 Years	32	$3,200,000

The compounding continues as long as the payments are reinvested. *Table 16-2 – Notes Accumulated* shows that if the income was reinvested for 50 years, the $100,000 invested would grow to $3.2 million without any additional capital!

WHO NEEDS THE BANK?

Table 16-3 - Note Amortization Schedule

Loan Amount $100,000.00	Term (months) 360	Interest Rate 6%	Monthly Payment $599.55
Year	Payments	Interest	Principal	Balance
1	$7,194.61	$5,966.59	$1,228.01	$98,771.99
2	$14,389.21	$11,857.45	$2,531.76	$97,468.24
3	$21,583.82	$17,667.89	$3,915.93	$96,084.07
4	$28,778.43	$23,392.96	$5,385.47	$94,614.53
5	$35,973.03	$29,027.39	$6,945.64	$93,054.36
6	$43,167.64	$34,565.59	$8,602.05	$91,397.95
7	$50,362.24	$40,001.63	$10,360.61	$89,639.39
8	$57,556.85	$45,329.20	$12,227.65	$87,772.35
9	$64,751.46	$50,541.62	$14,209.83	$85,790.17
10	$71,946.06	$55,631.79	$16,314.28	$83,685.72
11	$79,140.67	$60,592.15	$18,548.52	$81,451.48
12	$86,335.28	$65,414.72	$20,920.56	$79,079.44
13	$93,529.88	$70,090.98	$23,438.91	$76,561.09
14	$100,724.49	$74,611.91	$26,112.58	$73,887.42
15	$107,919.09	$78,967.94	$28,951.16	$71,048.84
16	$115,113.70	$83,148.89	$31,964.81	$68,035.19
17	$122,308.31	$87,143.96	$35,164.34	$64,835.66
18	$129,502.91	$90,941.70	$38,561.21	$61,438.79
19	$136,697.52	$94,529.92	$42,167.60	$57,832.40
20	$143,892.13	$97,895.71	$45,996.41	$54,003.59
21	$151,086.73	$101,025.35	$50,061.38	$49,938.62
22	$158,281.34	$103,904.27	$54,377.07	$45,622.93
23	$165,475.94	$106,517.00	$58,958.94	$41,041.06
24	$172,670.55	$108,847.14	$63,823.41	$36,176.59
25	$179,865.16	$110,877.24	$68,987.91	$31,012.09
26	$187,059.76	$112,588.82	$74,470.95	$25,529.05
27	$194,254.37	$113,962.21	$80,292.16	$19,707.84
28	$201,448.98	$114,976.55	$86,472.42	$13,527.58
29	$208,643.58	$115,609.72	$93,033.86	$6,966.14
30	$215,838.19	$115,838.19	$100,000.00	$0.00

CHAPTER 16 – WHAT IF I'M NOT READY TO RETIRE?

Besides turning a $100,000 investment into notes valued at $3.2 million dollars, the combined income on the 32 notes you'd own in 50 years would pay $19,185 per month for another 30 years!

Table 16-3 – Note Amortization Schedule illustrates how you and your family can benefit from the magic of compound interest the way that banks do. Just think of what is possible if you teach your grandchildren to steadily invest in notes throughout their lives. Leaving this type of legacy for your family will ensure that your picture will hang above the mantle for generations to come!

WHO NEEDS THE BANK?

17

What If I Need Income Now?

"The super rich have invested in businesses, real estate, art, and other assets. The income from these assets is now concentrating even faster than income from work."

— Robert Reich

WHO NEEDS THE BANK?

As Americans turn 65, quit their jobs, and start enjoying their "golden years," many realize that the income from their investments is not enough to support their lifestyle. According to the National Association of Home Builders, the average retiree in the United States holds 62% of their net worth in home equity. You can't afford to have nearly two-thirds of your life savings tied up in your home!

How much *income* does your house produce? The most common reply to this question is, "None" but a more accurate answer is, "Negative none" because besides producing no *income,* your home actually incurs *expenses* every month.

Those who achieve the American dream of paying off their home before retiring believe that when their mortgage is satisfied they'll be able to divert the money from their largest monthly expense to margaritas and travel!

Unfortunately, the retirement most people envision doesn't work out. People don't earn as much in retirement as they did while working. A substantial portion of their monthly Social Security or pension check must be set aside to pay the property tax, insurance, HOA dues, maintenance, and repairs for their home. So much for the margaritas and travel! Few people are able to enjoy the retirement lifestyle they saved their entire lives to achieve.

This problem is prevalent across the nation. After speaking at an event in San Diego, I was approached by a retired couple who'd been teachers for more than 40 years. Over several decades their home appreciated to over $1 million

CHAPTER 17 – WHAT IF I NEED INCOME NOW?

dollars in value. When they retired, they downsized and were able to use their equity to pay cash for a smaller home but the property tax takes all of the husband's monthly pension check and half of the wife's! They struggle to make ends meet and can't even afford a driving vacation! For them, the dream of home ownership has turned into a *nightmare!*

These people are perfect candidates for a reverse mortgage. These loans have been misunderstood for years, but if properly executed, they can be an awesome tool to leverage the equity in your home to substantially increase your cash flow in retirement. The first thing to understand is that the bank is NOT going to get your home when you die! If they do, that means they either gave you far more than you should have received or you lived decades longer than you were supposed to. Either way, you win!

Let's assume that your home is valued at $200,000 and you don't have a loan. If your taxes are $2,400 per year and the homeowner's insurance is $1,200, you must set aside $300/mo. from your monthly Social Security check to pay the $3,600 of *negative income* produced by your home.

The value of your home is the same whether you have a mortgage or not. If you obtain a reverse mortgage for $100,000 (half of your home's value), and invest the proceeds in a real estate note paying 5% interest, you'd receive $536.82 per month for the next 30 years, enough to pay the $300/mo. currently coming out of your Social Security check with $236.82 left over to spend as you please!

WHO NEEDS THE BANK?

The loan interest is accruing on *half* of your home's value, but appreciation is accruing on *all* of the home's value. Assuming appreciation of 3%, your $200,000 home would increase in value by $6,000 in the first year.

Because the reverse mortgage has no payments, the amount owed increases each month as interest accrues. If your loan is at 6%, the $100,000 loan balance would increase by $6,000, which means the appreciation offset the interest accrued and you broke even! The $536.82 monthly checks ($6,441.86 per year) didn't take any equity from your home! The key is to *invest* the cash from the reverse mortgage and eat the *interest*, rather than getting a loan and eating your *equity*!

If the $200,000 home in this example represents 62% of the owner's net worth, then their other assets, including checking, savings, IRAs, and stocks would be equal to 38% of their net worth ($122,580). If invested in a bank at 0.2%, the retiree would receive $245.16 *per year* which is only $20.43 per month, about enough for one Starbucks coffee a week!

If instead, you invested $100,000 of the $122,580 in a real estate note earning 5%; your income would increase from $20.43 to $536.82, a difference of $516.39 per month! Notes can vastly improve your lifestyle! Let's compare:

BEFORE
$1,200.00   Social Security income
+ $20.43   Bank interest
- $300.00   Property tax and insurance
$920.43   Expendable monthly income

CHAPTER 17 – WHAT IF I NEED INCOME NOW?

AFTER
$ 1,200.00   Social Security income
+ $536.82   Payment on note bought with reverse mortgage
+ $536.82   Payment on note bought with bank savings
- $300.00   Property tax and insurance
$1,973.64   Expendable monthly income

By investing their hard-earned savings in notes instead of keeping it in home equity or the bank, the retiree in this example more than doubled their expendable monthly income, with $1,053.21 more to spend each month! Do you think an extra $250.00 of spending money every week makes a difference in a retiree's lifestyle?

They would still live in the same house with the same neighbors, but just won't see them as often because they'll be out spending money and enjoying themselves instead of being homebound and house poor in their golden years!

If you plan to move in a few years, a reverse mortgage is probably not a good option for you. The loans are expensive to obtain because the fees are based on your home's value, not the loan amount. Unfortunately, since these loans pay higher commissions to loan officers than other loans, they sometimes attract dishonest lenders who are more interested in getting a large paycheck than doing what is best for you.

Be sure to find a reputable mortgage lender who specializes in reverse mortgages and will tell you if it's not the best option for you. That person in Tucson, AZ, is Tina Steele. I've known Tina for many years and can attribute all that I

WHO NEEDS THE BANK?

know about reverse mortgages to her! Besides being very knowledgeable, she is also very honest. It's important to get good advice, so ask around for an experienced and reputable lender who is a reverse mortgage expert.

18

What If I Need to Sell My Notes?

"About the time that we can make the ends meet, somebody moves the ends."

- Herbert Hoover

WHO NEEDS THE BANK?

Some home sellers offer to "carry back" financing for the buyers who purchase their home. Offering financing attracts buyers who for one reason or another cannot obtain a loan from a bank. Since few sellers are willing or able to offer financing, those who do will sell their homes faster, at a higher price, and earn a higher rate of interest than bank loans.

The promissory note is a borrower's written *promise to repay* the loan. The note contains information about the loan including the type of loan (amortized, simple, or interest-only), the loan amount, interest rate, repayment term, payment amount, and frequency in which payments are to be made. These terms are established when the note is originated and cannot be changed over the duration of the loan no matter how many times the loan is bought and sold.

After a promissory note is originated and signed by a borrower, the lien holder who funds the note can sell all or part of the payments to another person or entity. You can't cut up your home with a chainsaw and sell the individual pieces of the real estate, but with a note you can sell any portion of the cash flow! Banks do it all the time, as anyone who's had their mortgage sold can attest.

Since the terms can't be changed, it's important for those originating notes to establish terms other note buyers would be willing to accept if your situation changes and you need to sell the note. The value of a note depends on many factors, including the interest rate, remaining term, amount of the borrower's down payment, repayment history, and the loan-to-value ratio.

CHAPTER 18 – WHAT IF I NEED TO SELL MY NOTES?

Table 18-1 – Amortized Loan Balance shows the balance of a $75,000 loan at 5% interest over a 30-year term. At the start of the loan, the balance doesn't decrease very quickly because most of the $402.62 payment is interest and very little is applied toward principal.

Table 18-1 – Amortized Loan Balance

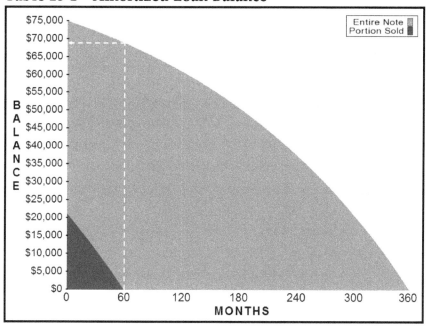

If the note holder wishes to immediately recover some of their $75,000 investment, they could sell 60 of the 360 payments to another note investor. If 60 payments of $402.62 are sold at a 5% yield, the note buyer would pay $21,335.12 to purchase them (shown in the dark triangle at lower left). The exact amount the note buyer pays can be easily determined using the Missing Value Calculator at www.NoteCarry.com, which is shown in *Table 18-2 – Note Buyer Yield of 5%*.

WHO NEEDS THE BANK?

Table 18-2 – Note Buyer Yield of 5%

Known Values		
Principal Value	$	$21335.12
Interest Rate	5 %	
Term(months)	60	
Monthly Payment	402.62	

By selling 60 of the 360 payments, the note holder recovers nearly 1/3 of their $75,000 investment, leaving just $53,664.88 invested. After 60 payments are paid to the note buyer, the note reverts back to the original note holder with a balance of $68,872.20 still owed by the borrower!

Over the first 60 payments, the borrower pays a total of $24,157.20 but only $6,127.80 is applied toward the principal, as indicated by the small triangular shape in the upper left of *Table 18-1 – Amortized Loan Balance*. When the loan comes back to the original note holder, the balance owed is $15,207.32 more than the $53,664.88 still invested in the deal!

What if the note holder can't find someone to buy the payments at a 5% yield and instead has to offer a 7% yield to sell the 60 payments? *Table 18-3 – Note Buyer Yield of 7%* shows that to obtain a yield of 7% the note buyer would pay $20,333.11 for 60 payments ($1,002.01 less than the $21,335.12 the note holder would receive at a 5% yield).

CHAPTER 18 – WHAT IF I NEED TO SELL MY NOTES?

Table 18-3 – Note Buyer Yield of 7%

	Known Values	
Principal Value	$	$20333.11
Interest Rate	7 %	
Term(months)	60	
Monthly Payment	402.62	

After the 60 payments have been made to the note buyer, the original note holder can sell off more payments (it doesn't have to be 60) or they can keep the monthly income for themselves. Because the term of the note is 360 payments, the note holder could sell off 60 payments *six times!*

Selling the payments is a good strategy for IRA accounts because you can immediately recoup a large portion of the money invested and use the proceeds from selling the payments to purchase more notes. When the note buyers have received all the payments you sold to them, the notes will all revert back to you and you'll have far more residual income than if you funded one note and didn't sell any payments.

WHO NEEDS THE BANK?

19

What If I Die Before I'm Repaid?

"You will only be remembered for two things: the problems you solve or the ones you create."

- Mike Murdock

WHO NEEDS THE BANK?

Several years ago, I met an energetic gentleman in his late 70s with a delightful sense of humor. He'd enjoyed a long career as a school teacher, but knew that the income from teaching wouldn't be enough to pay for the lifestyle he desired for his family.

Over his 40-year career, the teacher and his wife bought and paid off dozens of rental properties. They now spend much of the year traveling and were intrigued by my offer to show them how they could increase their monthly income while eliminating the hassle and expense of owning rentals.

Since most of their properties were owned free and clear, I suggested that they entertain the idea of selling the homes with financing. I explained that the properties would sell for a higher price and they'd continue to be paid every month for decades after the sale. They seemed somewhat interested and said they'd think about it.

We listed one of their rental properties and received two offers in the first week. The first offer of $115,000 was from a traditional buyer who intended to make a 3.5% down payment and obtain an FHA loan for the 96.5% balance.

The second offer of $125,000 came from an investor who owned multiple properties and wished to add to his rental portfolio. This buyer had a cash down payment of $25,000 (20%) and offered to purchase the property in "as-is" condition without any repairs if the sellers would finance the remaining $100,000 of the purchase price.

19 - WHAT IF I DIE BEFORE I'M REPAID?

Even though the offer from the investor was $10,000 higher, guaranteed that no repairs would be requested, and would pay 7% interest for decades, the sellers initially opted to accept the lower purchase price because they didn't want to carry a loan for 30 years.

When I asked why, the gentleman said with a smile, "I'll be *dead* by then! At 77 years old, I'm optimistic, but not *that* optimistic!" I asked how many people he knew who stayed in their home for 30 years. As I watched him process that question, I presented him with this scenario:

$ 25,000 Buyer's cash down payment
$ 90,000 1st position loan (funded by someone else)
$115,000 Cash at closing
$ 10,000 2nd position loan (carried by sellers)

I explained that between the buyer's down payment of $25,000 and the $90,000 from selling the loan to a retiree they would receive the same $115,000 offered by the first buyer and the $10,000 note in 2nd position was a *bonus!* What was their risk?

The concept of holding *paper* was new to the sellers and they didn't want the note, even if it was free! I assured the sellers that I could find someone to purchase the $10,000 note from them, but because there was no payment history and the note was in 2nd position, the value would likely be discounted by 50% to account for the added risk. I pointed out that even at a 50% discount they would receive $5,000 more for their property and not have to carry either note themselves.

WHO NEEDS THE BANK?

The sellers finally agreed to take the higher offer but the gentleman looked at me with a twinkle in his eye and said, "See if you can get $6,000 for the 2nd."

I didn't have to look far to find someone willing to pay $6,000.00 for the $10,000 note but the "someone" was my wife, Camille. She had cash to lend in her self-directed Roth IRA account, but was not eligible to buy the note because I was earning a real estate commission for selling the property.

The Internal Revenue Service (IRS) deems any income or personal benefit gained outside of a retirement account to be a "prohibited transaction." Although Camille would have liked to do the deal, we had to find someone else to buy the note.

A benefit of not using banks to fund loans is that deals can close much faster. The closing was fast approaching and I hadn't found another investor to buy the note. It occurred to me that if I had a debt of $10,000 that was being sold for $6,000 I'd want to buy it myself!

I asked the buyer's agent if the buyer would like to purchase the 2nd position loan at a discount and they jumped at the chance to save $4,000. We wrote an Addendum to decrease the sale price by $4,000 and increase the down payment by $6,000, removing the necessity for the 2nd note.

In this *win-win-win-win* deal the buyers got a $4,000 discount, the sellers got $6,000 more than they'd initially agreed to accept, the neighbors benefitted from a higher sale price, and I earned $7,500 for putting the deal together.

19 - WHAT IF I DIE BEFORE I'M REPAID?

Sometimes you have to get creative to make deals work, but if you put your mind to it, there's usually a solution that works for everyone.

I've met with dozens of people in their 70s who initially reject the idea of funding 30-year notes but later reconsider. After funding one note, they usually come back to fund many more because they can't find other investments that offer the security and high rate of return they get with notes.

Every family has at least one child who isn't good with money. These children would likely blow all their inheritance within a year and struggle financially for the rest of their life, but notes can provide your children and grandchildren with a monthly allowance that lasts for *decades* after you're dead!

I've helped countless investors build large portfolios of rental properties over their lifetime, only to have their children sell all the properties at a discount when they die. The children often appreciate the gesture but are either not interested in being landlords or want to use the money for something else.

If you hold notes in a trust with your heirs listed as successor beneficiaries, you'd receive the monthly payments until you die and then they'd automatically revert to your heirs. The borrowers would continue to send the same amount to the same legal entity (your trust), but the checks would be cashed by a different family member. Notes are a great way to leave a legacy for your family. You can improve the lives of your family for generations to come without turning your loved ones into landlords!

WHO NEEDS THE BANK?

20

Where Can I Find Notes to Fund?

"Surround yourself with the best people you can find, delegate authority, and don't interfere as long as the policy you've decided upon is being carried out."

- Ronald Reagan

WHO NEEDS THE BANK?

Note opportunities are everywhere! A note is created every time a property is purchased or sold (except for cash transactions). We've been trained to send borrowers to banks for loans, but what if the buyer can't qualify? The process is easier with private lenders, because we use *people* with common sense who want to live like rich bankers!

While at a conference in 2014, I contacted a college friend who I hadn't seen in more than twenty years. We met for breakfast one morning and began sharing the paths our lives had taken since graduation. During our visit, my friend asked about the real estate market in Arizona.

I told him that home prices had fallen by nearly 50% in the recession but were rising again and would continue to rise if more buyers could get loans. Banks were turning down nearly *half* the borrowers who applied for loans, but I was helping qualified buyers find retirees to finance their purchase.

The loans were for less than 80% of the home's value, the borrowers made a large down payment, and a licensed mortgage lender checked the credit and verified the borrower's ability to repay the loan.

My friend's face lit up and he asked, "If I had $50,000 in my retirement account could I buy a property from you?" When I said, "Yes," he told me that he'd owned a successful business for many years, but was 50 years old and hadn't saved very much for retirement.

20 – WHERE CAN I FIND NOTES TO FUND?

I found a property for him in less than a week! The sellers owned several rental properties but had been relocated out of state. They'd determined that they weren't coming back to Arizona but were disappointed by the market value of their properties at the time, stating that they'd lose money selling at those prices.

I proposed the idea of selling their properties with financing and being paid over time. With a higher sale price and years of interest they could easily recover the value lost to depreciation during the market downturn.

The next day the sellers called to tell me they liked the idea of being the bank. In fact, they liked it so much they asked if my friend with the $50,000 in his retirement account would buy *two* of their properties instead of one! We wrote up the offers for both properties and closed two weeks later!

Buyer Benefits

The value of both properties was $250,000 at the time. The $200,000 in loans was amortized over 15 years so the properties would be paid off just in time for my 50-year old friend to retire when he turned 65. The rents were enough to pay the expenses and still produce a small cash surplus.

Without factoring in the monthly cash flow, future increases in rent, or market appreciation, my friend's $50,000 investment would be worth $250,000, an increase of 500% in 15 years! His retirement will be better than expected because the properties have each appreciated by about $10,000 a year since he purchased them.

WHO NEEDS THE BANK?

Seller Benefits

The sellers stopped being absentee landlords, got $10,000 more on each property than they would have gotten in a traditional sale, and receive more each month than they could earn on other investments. The $100,000 they'll collect in interest on the 15-year loans is funding their children's college education!

This is a great example of how a little creativity can solve several problems at the same time. In addition to the obvious purchase and sale of real estate, this transaction provided the buyer with a secure retirement and the sellers with a college education for their children. I didn't go to breakfast with my friend that morning with the intention of selling homes, but was able to help two friends solve their problems by educating them about seller financing and real estate notes!

I received *four* real estate commissions for just a few hours of work, but a lot more went on behind the scenes. This deal was made possible by the time and money I've invested for years to educate myself and open my mind to new ideas. As a lifelong learner, I added value with my knowledge, not by opening the door for a home inspector.

There are dozens of Internet websites that offer platforms to buy and sell real estate notes, but be very careful buying notes from strangers, especially in out-of-state markets you know nothing about. If you had ten notes and were going to sell two, which would you sell; the two *worst* notes or the two *best* notes?

20 – WHERE CAN I FIND NOTES TO FUND?

There's lots of overpriced "junk" paper for sale backed by collateral that isn't worth as much as they're asking for the note. There are also scammers who will try to buy your notes for far less than a reputable investor would pay.

Camille and I follow two simple rules to limit our risk. First, we don't buy notes from strangers. We only buy from people we've known long enough to trust and who live in close proximity to the property we're investing in. The second rule is that our "boots on the ground" trusted partner is also invested in the property, so if something goes wrong they're incentivized to fix it or lose their equity.

If you're not a real estate agent or investor, that's okay and could actually be better. It's easier to fund real estate investments if you have consistent income from a steady monthly paycheck. Rather than trying to become a "jack of all trades" and an expert at none, I've surrounded myself with people who are experts at what they do so I can focus my efforts on the things that best utilize my skills.

If you're new to note investing, I suggest that you partner with someone who lives locally, has a good reputation, and already owns several real estate notes. This approach may not produce as high of a return but will familiarize you with the process while limiting your exposure and keeping you from buying someone else's bad notes.

If someone gave you this book, contact them to find out what local note investing opportunities might be available. You can also check **www.WhoNeedsTheBank.com** which is a website I've built to connect property owners around the country with note buyers who may be interested in purchasing their notes.

There are many creative ways to structure profitable deals, but simply knowing someone doesn't relieve you of the responsibility to perform due diligence. It's your job to ensure that basic protections are taken on each investment to preserve your capital. Use the information found in the next chapter to guide your investment decisions.

21

What Should I Look For In Notes?

"Our incomes are like our shoes; if too small, they gall and pinch us; but if too large, they cause us to stumble and to trip."

- John Locke

WHO NEEDS THE BANK?

We've covered a variety of topics and discussed many ways to protect your investment. Below, is a checklist of things to verify during the due diligence process before you fund a note. I encourage you to make your own list of the things you deem important to ensure that you're making a sound investment. These are things to look for in the origination:

ORIGINATION REQUIREMENTS

Licensed Mortgage Loan Originator – If originated by a MLO licensed in the state where the property is located, the note likely complies with state and federal lending laws.

Licensed Loan Servicer – If serviced from the start by a licensed servicing company, there's little chance that any laws have been broken or the repayment history has been altered.

Title Insurance – A lender's title policy issued when the note is funded guarantees the priority of the lien and protects the note holder from title claims and disputes over legal access.

Escrowed Property Taxes – Property taxes are prorated and collected by the loan servicer each month to insure the taxes stay current. A tax lien can wipe out a 1st position note!

Escrowed Hazard Insurance – The hazard insurance premium is paid by the loan servicer to ensure that the policy doesn't lapse and fire, wind, or water can't affect your collateral!

Collateral – Single Family Residences appeal to more buyers than commercial, multi-unit, or rural properties. If foreclosed on, they're easier to resell and therefore, they present less risk.

21 – WHAT SHOULD I LOOK FOR IN NOTES?

These are the items you should get with the collateral file:

DOCUMENTATION REQUIREMENTS

Original Note and Deed – After originating or purchasing a note, you should receive the original promissory note and deed for the property with blue ink signatures (copies are <u>not</u> okay). If serviced, verify that the servicer has the original documents.

Borrower's Payment History – If purchasing an existing note, you'll want to get a copy of the payment history to determine whether the payments are current and being made on time.

Original Closing Statement – Obtaining a copy of the original closing statement enables you to determine the down payment the borrower paid and the amount of "skin" they've invested.

Loan Servicing Agreement – If the note is professionally serviced, you'll want to review the terms of the servicing agreement and verify who is responsible for the servicing fees.

Complete Chain of Title – Whether a note has never been sold or assigned many times, you need a complete history with signed documentation each time the note changed ownership.

Borrower's Credit Report – It's important to have a copy of the borrower's credit and mortgage application to verify that the borrower had the ability to pay when the note was originated.

Verification of Title Insurance – A copy of the title insurance policy should be obtained to ensure that the note was covered by a lender's title policy when the note was originated.

WHO NEEDS THE BANK?

Insurance Policy – Obtain a copy of the hazard insurance policy to verify that the amount of coverage is enough to protect the collateral and that you are named as "also insured."

Property Tax Statement – Get a current copy of the property tax statement to ensure that the amount escrowed for taxes is enough to pay the bill and that the taxes are not in arrears.

Property Valuation – A broker price opinion, appraisal, or both should be obtained from a local real estate professional to verify the value provided by online valuation websites.

Market Conditions – Contact the local Chamber of Commerce and an experienced real estate broker to obtain information about unemployment, job creation, and market sentiment.

Community Demographics – If investing in another market, I use Wikipedia to obtain census data, find major employers, and determine if the population is increasing or decreasing.

Interest Rate – Check the usury laws in the state where the property is located to ensure that the interest rate doesn't exceed the legal rate allowed by law.

Loan to Value – Divide the amount remaining on the loan by the current market value of the property to determine the loan to value ratio and get a better understanding of the risk.

DODD-FRANK REQUIREMENTS

In a response to the 2008 financial crisis, the Dodd-Frank Wall Street Reform and Consumer Protection Act was signed

21 – WHAT SHOULD I LOOK FOR IN NOTES?

into law on July 21, 2010, and contains the most significant changes to financial regulation since the Great Depression.

The Dodd-Frank Act was passed to protect *consumers*, but in some cases, the protections were so severe that lenders stopped lending and borrowers were *protected* from ever obtaining a home! The restrictions don't affect loans made to investors or companies, but if you *originate* notes to owner-occupants (borrowers who intend to occupy the property), there are things you can't do. A summary of the restrictions contained in the Dodd-Frank legislation is provided below:

Ability to Repay – Lenders must make a good faith effort to ensure that borrowers can repay the debt and don't have more than 43% of their gross income going toward payment of debt.

Amortization – Loans must be fully amortized with principal and interest payments for no more than 30 years. Interest-only and negative amortizing loans are no longer allowed.

Balloon Payment – Sellers who fund only one loan per year can require an early payoff but the earliest a balloon payment can occur is five years after the loan is originated.

Home Builder – Corporations, LLCs, and individuals who construct a home in the normal course of their business cannot provide seller financing to the buyer of the home.

Variable Interest – The interest rate must be fixed for at least five years with reasonable annual and lifetime limits on how much the interest rate can increase.

WHO NEEDS THE BANK?

22

How Can I Get Started With Notes?

"Success is not a stop sign."

- Robert Kiyosaki

WHO NEEDS THE BANK?

Money is like closet space; no matter how much you have, it somehow disappears! Many people have their annual raise allocated to a new expense before it even appears in their paycheck. Those who win substantial amounts of money in a lottery often blow it all in a matter of months because they've never been taught to manage their money.

My father would get on his 'savings' soapbox once a year around 'raise time'. He'd ask his co-workers and employees, "Why do you need to spend more next week than you spent this week?" He'd plead with them to invest their raise for retirement so they'd never even miss the money being saved. Saving an upcoming pay increase before you actually receive it removes the temptation to find new ways to spend the money.

I took my father's advice and invested each raise into my 401(k) retirement plan. With each investment, I received an instant profit because my employer matched my contribution dollar for dollar on up to 4% of my gross earnings! I invested the additional income from each promotion and pay increase for 22 years and was able to quit my job at 42 years old!

I also adopted my father's enthusiasm for encouraging others to save. I carry on his legacy by encouraging others to put away at least half of their raise each year. One co-worker followed my example and invested it all. She amassed so much in her retirement account that I married her nearly a decade later (true story), but I did NOT marry Camille for her money! Investing each raise enabled me to retire 23 years early and Camille quit the high-paying job she hated on her 40th birthday (her parents and I picked her up in a limousine).

22 – HOW CAN I GET STARTED WITH NOTES?

If you invest just $25 (5 cups of coffee) from each two-week paycheck into your retirement account and increase it by $25 per paycheck every year, you'll be saving $100 from every check by the 4th year. After 20 years, you'll be putting away $500 from every paycheck and by the time you retire after 40 years, you'll be squirreling away $1,000 per paycheck without ever feeling any pain!

Assuming that you receive 26 paychecks per year and average a 5% return on your investments, the value of your $25 investments would grow to over *$1 million dollars* in 40 years. If you diversified by investing the $1,000,000 into a variety of real estate notes earning 5% interest, you'd receive monthly payments of $5,368 for 30 years after you retire!

That's how retirement is supposed to be, but most people never take the time to plan. Instead, they leave their money sitting in the bank earning 0.2% interest on the money it took them a lifetime to save!

Many people are shocked to discover that their largest investment (their home) produces *negative* income every month and that they'd actually be better off burying their money in a *hole* because holes don't have property tax! Homes tend to appreciate over time, which can offset the cost of maintenance, but appreciation is only realized when you *sell*, while the monthly expenses must be paid as they occur.

Unfortunately, few people are mentored by a passionate saver like my dad and an amazing budgeter like my mom. They don't make an intentional plan for saving regularly and

WHO NEEDS THE BANK?

thus never get around to saving at all! Their lack of planning and inability to save usually means that they'll be unable to enjoy their retirement because they never set firm goals and took action to accomplish them.

Many retirees find themselves in this predicament. Although they tried to save, bills got in the way throughout their lives. For most, the fifty-year debt cycle started in high school when they borrowed money to purchase a car to commute to and from work. After leaving home for college, they became responsible for their own food, lodging, utilities, furniture, clothing, supplies, etc.

As their knowledge and skill became more valuable in the workplace, their income increased but eating out, hobbies, sporting events, concerts, and other things they enjoyed all required money. When they fell in love, money was spent on travel, gifts, and romantic weekends together.

A wedding eventually followed, which meant finding a larger place to live. The additional square footage required more furniture, draperies, appliances, and home décor, as well as higher taxes, home owners insurance, utility bills, association fees, and mortgage payments.

Once settled, they started families and had new expenses for daycare, diapers, healthcare, etc. Each pay raise was quickly consumed by new expenses like hockey skates, ballerina slippers, karate lessons, doll houses, and gymnastics classes.

22 – HOW CAN I GET STARTED WITH NOTES?

After eighteen years of never-ending bills, their children finally graduated high school and left home for college, but due to the high cost of tuition, many felt obligated to help their children with the expense. This was also the case with weddings, which can also be very expensive.

When the children were finally educated, married, and gainfully employed with a home of their own, their parents took a huge sigh of relief, but then the grandchildren came and the entire cycle started over!

It's very easy to become so caught up in life that you're unable to save. This is why it's so important to get the highest return possible on the money you're able to put away. The bank is not the answer!

WHO NEEDS THE BANK?

23

Why Do I Need To Start Right Away?

"If you are the kind of person who is waiting for the 'right' thing to happen, you might wait for a long time. It's like waiting for all the traffic lights to be green for five miles before starting the trip."

- Robert Kiyosaki

WHO NEEDS THE BANK?

If you don't take charge of your life, your fate will be determined by your kids or the government. Corporate America once offered the 40-40-40 retirement plan in which you worked 40 hours a week for 40 years and retired with a pension equal to 40% of your salary. Few employers still offer pensions but may encourage retirement saving by offering a 401(k) match, but if you don't save, they don't *match!*

If you work for an employer who will match your savings, you should be investing as much as they'll match because you'll immediately earn a 100% return on your money! The government adds even more incentive to save by making your 401(k) investments tax deductible. When you put money away for retirement, you'll get an income tax deduction!

For example, an investment of $100 is immediately matched with $100 from your employer. If you're in a 20% income tax bracket, the tax deduction reduces the amount you owe for income tax by $20, so it really only costs you $80 to save $200 and the money grows tax-free until you retire.

Starting a 401(k) is easy; just have your employer deduct $50 from each paycheck. If you can't afford $50 then start with $25, $15, or $10, but *start* with whatever you can manage! Drinking water instead of soft drinks is healthier and you'll be on your way to financial health too.

The average American family has about 2% of their income left over after all their monthly bills have been paid. The unallocated income remaining is called *discretionary income* because it isn't needed to pay bills and how you spend the

23 – WHY DO I NEED TO START RIGHT AWAY?

money is at your discretion. You don't want to blow your discretionary income on frivolous things because you have to earn $100.00 for every $2.00 of discretionary income left over. When all but 2% of your income is committed to bills, you have to earn $2,500.00 to buy just $50.00 of discretionary items.

What if you're a good money manager and are able to save 10% of your gross pay after all your bills are paid? This is five times more than the average person saves, but consider this: if you have 10% of your gross pay at your discretion, you must earn $50.00 to purchase a $5.00 cup of coffee, $500.00 to put $50.00 worth of gas in your car, $5,000.00 to buy a $500.00 smart phone, $50,000.00 to take a $5,000.00 vacation and $500,000.00 to purchase a $50,000.00 car!

Because it takes so much earned income to create discretionary income, the money you save should be treated like a family heirloom! An effective way to curb spending on frivolous items is to multiply every purchase by a factor of 10.

A concert T-shirt doesn't seem quite as desirable when the price goes from $30.00 to $300.00 and the premium cable channels lose their appeal when the price goes from $100.00 to $1,000.00 a month. How many time shares would you buy if the price was $350,000.00 instead of $35,000.00? To help curb spending on impulse purchases write 'X10' on Post It® notes and stick them on your cash, check book, and credit cards!

Saving money is a start, but keeping your money working is what's most important! *Table 23-1 – Compound Interest on*

WHO NEEDS THE BANK?

$100,000 Investment illustrates the impact the last three years of a 30-year period can make on your investments.

Table 23-1 – Compound Interest on $100,000 Investment

Year	5%		10%	
	Interest	Balance	Interest	Balance
1	$5,000	$105,000	$10,000	$110,000
3	$5,513	$115,763	$12,100	$133,100
5	$6,078	$127,628	$14,641	$161,051
7	$6,700	$140,710	$17,716	$194,872
10	$7,757	$162,889	$23,579	$259,374
15	$9,900	$207,893	$37,975	$417,725
20	$12,635	$265,330	$61,159	$672,750
25	$16,125	$338,635	$98,497	$1,083,471
26	$16,932	$355,567	$108,347	$1,191,818
27	$17,778	$373,346	$119,182	$1,310,999
28	$18,667	$392,013	$131,100	$1,442,099
29	$19,601	$411,614	$144,210	$1,586,309
30	$20,581	$432,194	$158,631	$1,744,940
Last 3 Years	$58,849		$433,941	

If you kept your money invested 90% of the time and lost just 36 days of interest each year (10%) for 30 years, you would

23 – WHY DO I NEED TO START RIGHT AWAY?

lose three years of interest. The lost revenue would total $59,849 if you're earning 5% interest and $433,941 at 10%.

How is it even possible to lose *four times more* than you originally invested? Unfortunately, the loss you experience is the interest during the last three years of the 30-year period when the balance is the highest.

Compound interest only works if your money is *invested* so don't hold out for *unicorn* loans with pie in the sky returns (they don't exist). Get your money invested at a sustainable rate of return and let the magic of compound interest do the rest! The longer you wait to invest, the more it will cost you. People spend their lives working for their money instead of letting their money work for them. Work smarter, not harder!

WHO NEEDS THE BANK?

24

How Can I Learn More About Notes?

"The secret to winning is constant, consistent management."
- Tom Landry

WHO NEEDS THE BANK?

My first experience with seller financing and real estate notes came in 2001 when we purchased a run-down trailer park with two other couples. The park was filled with small retro trailers from the 1950s that had dark paneling, shag carpet, and appliances from an episode of The Flintstones. Banks wouldn't lend on the property, so we acquired the property with carry-back financing from the seller.

Over the next three years, we replaced the 1950s homes with 1980s park model homes that we acquired from retirees. The clean, well-maintained units had carports and modern amenities that brought higher monthly rents and attracted a different class of tenants who owned cars and had jobs! We installed separate electric meters and converted the furnace, water heater, and stove in each unit to propane so the tenants would be responsible for paying their own utilities.

Selling the property proved to be easy, but getting it closed was a different story. As illustrated in Table 24-1 – *Trailer Park Sale History*, we had the property in escrow three times but the buyers all cancelled because they couldn't get financing. We'd purchased the park with seller financing and it became apparent that we'd have to offer financing to sell it.

After trying to sell for a year, we listed the park with seller financing and it sold in just 21 days. The buyer was a surgeon who paid $135,000 down and we created a note for the remaining $335,000. Within a month of selling the property, I started getting postcards from investors who wanted to buy our note. At first I ignored them, but we finally sold the note to a note buyer after holding it for just six months.

24 – HOW CAN I LEARN MORE ABOUT NOTES?

Table 24-1 – Trailer Park Sale History

2500032	Closed	$470,000	-1.1%	03/08/2005	61
+	Closed	$475,000		03/08/2005	65
+	Pending	$475,000		01/23/2005	21
+	Contingent	$475,000		01/23/2005	21
+	New	$475,000		01/01/2005	0
2417994	Expired	$475,000	-5.0%	01/01/2005	171
+	Expired	$475,000		12/31/2004	172
+	Active	$475,000		11/23/2004	134
+	Back On Market	$475,000		11/23/2004	134
+	Pending	$475,000		10/07/2004	86
+	Contingent	$475,000		10/07/2004	86
+	Price Change	$475,000	-5.0%	08/31/2004	49
+	New	$499,900		07/12/2004	0
2406159	Expired	$499,900	-3.9%	07/13/2004	129
+	Expired	$499,900		07/12/2004	130
+	Price Change	$499,900	-2.9%	04/16/2004	42
+	New	$515,000		03/04/2004	0
2323299	Expired	$520,000	153.7%	03/04/2004	153
+	Expired	$520,000		03/03/2004	157
+	Active	$520,000		02/21/2004	145
+	Back On Market	$520,000		02/21/2004	145
+	Pending	$520,000		02/20/2004	144
+	Contingent	$520,000		02/20/2004	144
+	Price Change	$520,000	-2.8%	01/23/2004	116
+	Price Change	$535,000	-2.7%	11/03/2003	35
+	New	$550,000		09/28/2003	0
2113867	Closed	$205,000		09/05/2001	57

I was surprised to find that it was much easier to sell the "paper" than it was the property! From this experience in 2005,

WHO NEEDS THE BANK?

I learned that seller financing enables you to sell faster and without bank hassles. Note buyers like borrowers with plenty of "skin" in the game." A substantial down payment lowers the loan-to-value ratio for the note investor and the monthly payment for the borrower, thus reducing the risk of default.

Seller financing has grown in popularity as more and more buyers can't obtain bank financing. Privately financed notes can create win-win deals if the borrowers and lenders understand the expectations of each other and everything is documented in a written agreement.

Laws vary from state to state, so be sure to seek the advice of a local licensed attorney who specializes in the type of transaction you're interested in funding before you enter into a deal.

In 2012, I created software that could quickly structure seller carry-back deals. I didn't build it to *sell*; I built it for me because I was running the same calculations over and over on each deal. I created a website for the software so the agents on my team could use it, but couldn't take my intellectual property with them when they left the company. In 2014, I demonstrated the software at my annual charity conference and **www.NoteCarry.com** was born!

Since then, hundreds of subscribers across the United States have used NoteCarry.com software to help people in their community buy and sell homes, save their credit, multiply their retirement income, and improve their lives.

24 – HOW CAN I LEARN MORE ABOUT NOTES?

In less than a minute, users can create worksheets to show buyers, sellers, and retiree investors how they'll benefit from the deal. The website is a work in progress as I'm continually adding new tools as different scenarios arise.

In addition to the software tools on **www.NoteCarry.com**, I also host weekly training webinars to share best practices and educate members of different investment strategies to achieve their financial goals. I've helped members across the country structure deals and NoteCarry Network members often fund deals for other members on the LIVE webinars each week! The online video library contains all of the weekly webinars recorded since 2015.

I speak at several note-investing conferences around the country and host my own conference once a year to share all that I've learned about real estate, finances, and life. After attending my conference, you'll never think about investing the same way again! If you want to learn how to find and fund notes and meet some of the smartest note investors in the country, you won't want to miss this event! Go to: **www.NoteBusinessBuilder.com**.

We've donated 100% of the proceeds from this event to the Make-A-Wish Foundation ever since we hosted our first event in 2009. I have a goal to donate $1 million dollars before I die and we're about halfway there but I need your help to achieve my goal, so educate yourself and help a child with a life-threatening illness at the same time! Get registered!

WHO NEEDS THE BANK?

25

Note Investing Success Story

"Today, if you look at financial systems around the globe, more than half the population of the world, three billion people, do not qualify to take out a loan from a bank. This is a shame."

- Muhammad Yunus

WHO NEEDS THE BANK?

In 2013, my bookkeeper's parents expressed an interest in purchasing a rental property. They'd retired and recently sold their home, which left them with a large sum of cash in their checking account. They needed a much better return than their bank was paying without restricting their ability to travel and enjoy retirement.

I explained how note investing could provide the higher return they were looking for without the responsibility or hassles of rental property that could impede their ability to travel. They were interested in avoiding the cost of property management, property tax, insurance, maintenance, repair, vacancy and HOA expenses, and especially the headaches of dealing with tenants. Their investment strategy was converted from tenants and toilets to *mailbox money!*

They purchased a home needing minor repairs, and spent about $5,000 on paint, carpet, faucets, and fixtures. Instead of becoming landlords as they'd initially planned, I resold their updated home 42 days later to a credit-challenged buyer who paid $35,000 more than they'd invested in the home.

The buyers were living in a one-bedroom apartment with their daughter and two dogs. The wife was a teacher and the husband worked as an HVAC technician. He'd recently changed jobs and couldn't qualify for a bank loan. I was impressed by the work ethic of this young man who often had to meet late in the evening because he worked until 9:00 PM.

The buyers fell in love with the newly-renovated three-bedroom home with a fenced yard for their dogs and a garage.

NOTE INVESTING SUCCESS STORY

They'd saved $7,000 for the down payment but the sellers wanted a down payment of $15,000.

I shared with the sellers how impressed I was with the buyer's work ethic and that he was earning thousands of dollars in commission each month on the HVAC equipment he sold. After meeting the buyers, the sellers agreed to finance $6,000 of the down payment in a separate note with 12 monthly payments of $500 in addition to the other notes.

To help the couple obtain the last $2,000 for their down payment, I hired the buyer to replace the air conditioner at a rental property we owned, which was about to become vacant. The note for the buyer to install an air conditioner on our rental property was in 4th position!

The *5th position* note was not anticipated, but the excited buyers had used their available cash to buy a new bedroom set for their daughter before realizing they needed to pay $1,000 for escrow and title fees. I provided them with another note for the $1,000 they were short in 5th position and they became home owners in June, 2013!

In July, the air conditioner was installed on our rental property as promised and in September they repaid the $1,000 loan so I returned the signed 4th and 5th position notes to them. A year later they made the final payment on the 3rd position note for $6,000 of the down payment.

Prior to owning, the buyers were paying $700 a month in rent with nothing to show for the $8,400 spent annually. After

WHO NEEDS THE BANK?

20 months of frugal living, they paid off three loans and had $30,000 in home equity! The garage in the new home enabled the industrious buyer to start his own HVAC repair business and he now has two employees working for him!

The buyers called a few years later on Christmas to thank me for giving them the opportunity of home ownership. They said it was hard at first, but they got used to paying the extra $500 per month and when that loan was repaid, they began adding an extra $500 to their truck payment. Besides paying off the air conditioner note, the closing cost note, and the down payment note, they also paid off their vehicle two years early!

It's sad that banks can no longer consider the potential that I saw in this industrious young couple. When given the opportunity, they were able to change their habits to achieve their dreams! They've continued to save and now own two rental properties which were also seller-financed.

When people ask what I'll do when I retire, I reply, "I'm already doing it!" Stories like this that change people's lives are why I love doing what I do!

Pay It Forward!

Bob Zachmeier

HOW TO FIND OUT MORE ABOUT NOTES

If you've enjoyed reading this book, please share it with others and go to: **www.amazon.com/Bob-Zachmeier/e/B0044P1EIY** to leave a favorable review.

If you'd like to purchase my software which enables you to structure seller-financed deals in your area in under a minute, go to: **www.NoteCarry.com**.

If you'd like more information about note investing or would like to test drive the weekly mentoring webinars I host for the NoteCarry Network, send an e-mail to **bob@notecarry.com**.

For information about my annual note-investing conference, go to **www.NoteBusinessBuilder.com** and get registered! If you'd like to purchase recordings from previous conferences, send an e-mail to bob@notecarry.com.

If you'd like to find seller-financed homes in markets across the United States, go to: **www.WhoNeedsTheBank.com** to start shopping or to add your property to the website!

For information about books written by Bob Zachmeier, visit: **www.OutOfTheBoxBooks.com** or just send an e-mail to: bob@notecarry.com.

WHO NEEDS THE BANK?

ABOUT THE AUTHOR

Bob Zachmeier was born and raised in Mandan, North Dakota. His parents taught by example that determination and a strong work ethic could achieve almost any goal. As the third of six children, Zachmeier learned to become self-reliant. He started a fireworks business at the age of 16 with billboard and radio advertising. The business helped to fund his college education and that of his sisters.

He became a part-time real estate agent in 2000 at the age of 40. In 2002, he was earning enough from real estate investments to leave his job and end a twenty-two-year career in the defense electronics industry. In 2004, Zachmeier and his wife, Camille, founded the Win3 Team in Tucson, Arizona. The name reflects their desire to create *win-win-win* situations for their clients, their company, and their community. They've raised over $500,000 for the Make-A-Wish Foundation and have received several philanthropic awards.

After the Great Recession of 2008, Zachmeier observed that several hard-working clients were having trouble qualifying for bank financing. He began helping them find funding from friends, family, and past clients who needed better returns than they earned at the bank. He created software to easily structure seller-financed deals and his website, **www.NoteCarry.com** offers hundreds of hours of training and software tools that teach his mentoring students how to help the buyers, sellers, and retirees in their community.

By sharing his experience and practical advice as a real estate broker, coach, college instructor, author, lecturer, and note investor, Bob Zachmeier has helped thousands of people improve their financial well-being. He has written and published six books; *Upside Up Real Estate Investing, Sold On Change!, Answers From Experts on Buying a Home, Answers From Experts on Selling a Home, A Daily Difference* and *Who Needs the Bank?*

CPSIA information can be obtained
at www.ICGtesting.com
Printed in the USA
LVHW092133180419
614769LV00001B/165/P